"Community. Generosity. Risk-taking. Action. Selflessness. Relationship. Brokenness—all of it encompassing the good news. It's good news that Seay, in *The Gospel According to Jesus*, poignantly tells us should be contagious and, best of all, liberating. Chris gets it. So should all of us."

— Mark Batterson, Lead Pastor,
National Community Church;
Best-selling Author, *In A Pit with
A Lion on a Snowy Day.*

"In his inimitable way, Seay reminds us that living the gospel is about transformation, not Sunday-school religion. It's a truth we should never tire of hearing."

— Matthew Barnett, Senior Pastor,
L. A. Dream Center.

"Chris Seay is one of my favorite people. He's a shepherd at heart. His insights on culture always take me into a better understanding of the world we live in. I'm grateful for him in so many ways."

— Donald Miller, Author,
Blue Like Jazz and *A Million Miles
in a Thousand Years*

THE
GOSPEL
ACCORDING
TO
JESUS

THE
GOSPEL
ACCORDING
TO
JESUS

CHRIS SEAY

THOMAS NELSON
Since 1798

NASHVILLE   DALLAS   MEXICO CITY   RIO DE JANEIRO

Published in Nashville, Tennessee, by Thomas Nelson. Thomas Nelson is a registered trademark of Thomas Nelson, Inc.

Thomas Nelson, Inc., titles may be purchased in bulk for educational, business, fund-raising, or sales promotional use. For information, please e-mail SpecialMarkets@ThomasNelson.com.

Library of Congress Cataloging-in-Publication Data

Seay, Chris.
    The Gospel according to Jesus / Chris Seay.
      p. cm.
    Includes bibliographical references (p.   ).
    ISBN 978-0-8499-4816-9 (hardcover)
    1. Christian life. I. Title.
BV4501.3.S42 2010
248.4—dc22   2010021300

Printed in the United States of America

10 11 12 13 14 QG 5 4 3 2 1

To my parents, Ed and Cindy Seay

As we swam through seas polluted by religion,
self-importance, and hypocrisy, you led me to encounter
the love of Jesus. I could not be more grateful.

Contents

ONE

Righteousness or Righteousness?

I like your Christ. I do not like your Christians. Your Christians are so unlike your Christ.
    –Mohandas Karamchand Gandhi

When the church and people of faith are at our best, it is an absolute thing of beauty.

You know what I am talking about, right? You have friends who serve King Jesus by caring for foster children, who love them selflessly despite anger and behavior issues that sometimes come with children from troubled beginnings. Or maybe you know a teacher who understands that teaching means having a deep love for the total well-being of her students, who instructs with a passion that could only come from her Creator. I have been blessed to see real Christianity up close, and I often feel like Moses with my face aglow as I catch a glimpse of God at work. You can rest assured that God is at work in this world, and his called-out people were made to reveal his glory and splendor in just these ways. After witnessing those who live out a life like Christ's, we are often left wondering why the church does not constantly live in this state and why our lives seem to touch this amazing healing power only rarely, although we stretch and strive for it just like the bleeding woman who reached for the hem of Jesus' tunic.

The truth is that many of us live in a dry, mundane wilderness of habitual failures and repeated mistakes. The promised land of grace and abundance is a distant dream, and we miss the miracles that surround us each day. It is easy to mock the children of Israel who grumbled and complained to God in the desert. *How could these people be so ungrateful?* we think. We feel like telling them, "God is giving you water from rocks and raining down miracle bread to feed you in the desert. Do you not see the miracle happening right before your eyes? God is providing all that you need and is leading you to a place of hope and abundance."

But we are more like the children of Israel than we are willing to admit. Most of us live at a level of luxury and indulgence that is unprecedented in all of history. Yet we too often focus on the few things we do not have. Like the children of Israel, we seem to be chasing our tails in the desert and missing the life that God has promised for us. But Scripture makes clear that as our minds are transformed, we will be transformed, and as we are transformed, our lives will bring God great pleasure. Paul wrote:

> Brothers and sisters, in light of *all I have shared with you about* God's mercies, I urge you to offer your bodies as a living and holy sacrifice *to God*, a sacred offering that brings Him pleasure; this is your reasonable, essential worship. Do not allow this world to mold you in its own image. Instead, be transformed *from the inside out* by renewing your mind. As a result, you will be able to discern what

God wills and whatever God finds good, pleasing, and complete. (Rom. 12:1–2)

What kind of lives do you imagine will bring great pleasure to God? Do lives that garner the respect of the religious establishment give God great pleasure? What about lives that seek comfort, protect personal wealth, and value personal safety above all else? Is it pleasing to God if we care for the poor, sick, and oppressed, and seek a social gospel? Is God excited about denominational loyalty, partisan politics, or pious appearance? Does God desire any of this? Is it possible that we have ignored Jesus—our wild, messianic King—and chosen to re-create Jesus in the image of the Pharisees themselves?

I believe that we all have some profound misunderstandings about faith—that there are places where we've misread the Scriptures, and that misunderstanding is clouding our way. So here is my primary question: What if we, the church, were so uninformed about basic foundational teachings of the historic Christian faith that most of us could not even attempt to articulate the gospel?

It would be a macabre indicator of our health, wouldn't it? Imagine this: a church where the majority of people are either completely unfamiliar with the most essential tenets of the Christian faith or—worse—they have wholly misunderstood them.

I am sure that all of us have sensed, at one point or another, a great disappointment with the state of the church today. We read the book of Acts and see the world being transformed through a group of ordinary people who are totally devoted to the way of Jesus, and we long to experience the same. We read the stories of Jesus feeding thousands with just a handful of food, healing the sick, and commissioning the disciples to do likewise. In fact, he says that when he departs, we (those who follow Jesus' way) will do even greater things. Is he kidding? We live in a world ravaged by both extreme poverty and extreme wealth, and it is hard for us to see the miraculous work of God in most of it. Didn't Jesus also pray that we would be one, just as he is one with the Father (John 17:22)? Yet, the church is splintered into thousands of fractious groups, and we live in a world so plagued by selfishness that the rich do not effectively offer any of their excess wealth to stop the needless and preventable deaths among our poorer brothers and sisters. Ralph Winter describes the problem this way:

> The underdeveloped societies suffer from one set of diseases: tuberculosis, malnutrition, pneumonia, parasites, typhoid, cholera, typhus, etc. Affluent America has virtually invented a whole new set of diseases: obesity, arteriosclerosis, heart disease, stroke, lung cancer, venereal disease, cirrhosis of the liver, drug addiction, alcoholism, divorce, battered children, suicide, murder. Take your choice. Labor-saving machines have turned out to be body-killing devices. Our affluence has allowed both mobility and isolation of the nuclear family, and as a result our divorce courts, our prisons and our mental institutions are flooded. In saving ourselves we have nearly lost ourselves.[1]

The church is the answer to this crisis, and though she is struggling to find her voice in this fractured world, she is no less the bride of Christ, beloved by Jesus the King. Somewhere along the way, she has lost the sense of awe and wonder of her salvation. But what is lost can be restored.

Avert Crisis or Engage?

I have spent much of the last decade working on a unique Bible project called *The Voice*. As I worked with many scholars, pastors, and gifted writers, I also took a great deal of time to discuss important translation choices (for words such as *baptism*, *Christ*, and *righteousness*) with a broad Christian audience. In many instances, it became clear that our translation could potentially be unsuccessful in leading the reader to a greater depth of understanding, despite the fact that we had technically chosen the right word. In fact, a word could be chosen (and be accurate, according to the dictionary) to translate a concept from the Greek or Hebrew, but the general perception of that word in the broader public could be absolutely incorrect. Language is fluid and important, so I spent an increasing amount of time seeking feedback about the most important words used most often in Scripture and what people actually believe these words mean.

I was astounded to learn that the Greek word translated as "righteousness," a word that appears more than 180 times in the New Testament, is totally misunderstood by Christians. It seemed that more than 90 percent of people, many who considered themselves students of the Bible, equated righteousness with morality or personal piety. As I listened to people elaborate, it became clear that the righteousness the majority of Christians are "seeking first" was not biblical righteousness at all. In fact, it was more like the righteousness of the Pharisees (read: self-righteousness). This is a major problem. No wonder the church was so self-righteous and condescending!

So if, as many believe, the book of Romans is the most critical book in the biblical canon to inform readers with a full and healthy understanding of the gospel, and in that book the central concept, presented 40 times, is *righteousness*, what might happen if the common meaning of the word *righteousness* was entirely misunderstood by a majority of Christians? The short answer: the church would have a different gospel and would be missing a fundamental truth of the gospel according to Jesus.

To see if my concerns were founded, I commissioned Barna Research Group to get some quantifiable data from more than one thousand American adults about their level of understanding of the term *righteousness* as used in the Bible: 18 percent said they had not heard the term *righteousness*; only 38 percent said they were very familiar with the term. Their answers confirmed my worst fears. How could someone be a Christian and not be familiar with the term *righteousness*? I thought there must have been many in this group who were marginal Christians, so I asked Barna to isolate the responses of those who attended church at least once a week. I was sure that this would make a difference. It did not. Among active churchgoers (who attend church at least once a week), 16 percent said they had not heard of the term and only 45 percent were very familiar with it. *This*, I thought, *is a damning indictment of the church.* But the data kept getting worse when I read the way the 45 percent of people familiar with the term actually defined *righteousness*.

If Jesus Were Preaching, Would You Pay Attention?

Jesus pulled together the greatest sermon ever preached, his Sermon on the Mount, with a clear call to action: "Seek first the kingdom of God and His righteousness, and then all these things will be given to you *too*" (Matt. 6:33). I wondered how many people possessed an adequate understanding of this text, so I asked the following question in the Barna survey:

> Q: In the Bible there is a quotation from Jesus that says, "Seek first the kingdom of God and His righteousness." What do you believe Jesus is referring to by *righteousness*?

Here are the answers from those who claimed to be familiar with the term *righteousness*:

What Christians Think It Means to "Seek First the Kingdom and His Righteousness" *% among those familiar with the term righteousness*		
First response	**All Christians**	**Active Churchgoers**
Holiness	32%	37%
Faithfulness	29	28
Morality	17	14
Justice	6	6
Beauty	2	3
Something else	6	6
Not sure	7	6
Total responses *% among those familiar with the term*	*695*	*426*
All responses	**All Christians**	**Churchgoers**
Holiness	52%	58%
Faithfulness	53	54
Morality	35	34
Justice	26	28
Beauty	14	15
Something else	7	7
Not sure	7	6
Total responses	*695*	*426*

They Will Know You by Your . . .

One of my concerns that arose from the Barna survey was the fact that many perceived *righteousness* as being about religious acts. In fact, the top response to the open-ended question, "What is righteousness?" was *morality*, to do the good and right thing. Sadly, most other answers seemed to be a variation on this theme. Paul is very clear in the book of Romans that our focus must not be on the tireless struggle to do the right thing; that will only exhaust us. The law and the rules are a constant reminder of our failure to deal with our sinful nature through our own wills. But a miraculous thing happens when we fix our attention on King Jesus and his kingdom: God begins to work out his righteousness through us.

There is a pop philosopher of our time who has articulated this struggle with sin quite well—this musician has developed a reputation as a first-class narcissist. I don't agree with much of what he says, and he may be a real jerk, but his music often makes me smile and nod my head. If he can grasp these truths, then I can assure you that each of us can as well. In his song "Addiction," Kanye sings (in a half-singing, half-rapping sort of way), "Why everything supposed to be bad make me feel so good? / Everything they told me not to is exactly what I would . . ." I think Kanye articulates what the apostle Paul expressed with heartfelt clarity:

This is what we know: the law comes from the spiritual realm. *My problem is that* I am of the fallen human realm, owned by sin, *which tries to keep me in its service. Listen,* I can't explain my actions. Here's why: I am not able to do the things I want; and at the same time I do the things I despise. If I am doing the things I have already decided not to do, I am agreeing with the law regarding what is good. But now I am no longer the one acting—*I've lost control*—sin has taken up residence in me *and is wreaking havoc.* I know that in me, that is, in my fallen human nature, there is nothing good. I can will myself to do something good, but that does not help me to carry it out. I can determine that I am going to do good, but I don't do it; instead, I end up living out the evil that I decided not to do. If I end up doing the exact thing I pledged not to do, I am no longer doing it because sin has taken up residence in me. (Rom. 7:14–20)

I can't help but do what I'm not supposed to do, especially if I know I'm not supposed to do it. Then I really want to do it. If we live out Christianity as a set of rules, our lives will become miserable failures.

Growing up in the church, I inherited a lot of this kind of faith, and I remember being at my church in Humble, Texas, where one Wednesday we had an hour-long talk about avoiding drugs. "Don't do drugs! Don't do drugs!" I am pretty sure that half the people there had never given drugs a second thought. But after thinking about drugs for an hour, you know what happened? Everyone left there thinking about doing drugs.

The next Wednesday I walked into the same room, where one week ago we had this drug talk, and there, just before our Wednesday-night church dinner, two of my church friends were huffing paint. Their heads were stuck in plastic bags, and they emerged with paint droplets on their faces. At that point I realized, *Something is deeply broken here.* I stood there wondering what made them want to do that. Then the pieces began to come together. The forceful talk about drugs the week before actually had the capacity to bring out the worst in them.

I was no Bible scholar in my teen years, but it did not take me long to realize that Paul was warning us in Romans about this very temptation and asking us to place our eyes in the direction of our King rather than focusing on our struggle with sin. This made sense. You can likely sense these same patterns in your own life, and you can see that a version of Christianity that is seeking first to "keep the rules" is on a collision course with our sinful nature. It will end in destruction, not the joy of salvation.

I tried to explain to the church leaders that the "Don't do this!" approach was not working, but my articulation of Paul was not well received by the church establishment, and their focus on following the rules seemed to grow into an obsession. Long lists were being created before my eyes. "This is what Christians should not do, so don't do it. Rule #1: Cut your hair lest you become a sinful hippie. Rule #2: Don't get pierced or tattooed; God hates that. Rule #3: Burn your records; that secular music is destroying your soul." And the list grew faster than Pinocchio's nose. We were focused on rules, rules, and more rules. As the rules increased, our desire to violate these rules grew as well. There was very little Jesus; there was very little grace. And there was very little discipleship.

Remember those rock-and-roll seminars of the 1980s that Christians used to promote? (They were usually called "The God of Rock" or something like that.) They were an astonishing spectacle. A so-called authority on rock music, who apparently had enough time on his hands to wear out hundreds of record needles running the Beatles' records in reverse, would spend an amazing amount of time listening to rock music, transcribing lyrics, and then listening to the music backward at a thousand different tempos in order to piece together hidden messages that most often were not there. Then he would travel to hundreds of churches and issue the list of the most offensive and destructive music in the culture. You know what happened after that, right? My friends went out and bought all the music on that blacklist.

There was one kid who sat in on one of these seminars at a Christian high school in Ohio who realized the same thing I realized: if you can get on the blacklist in a Christian rock seminar, a lot of those Christian kids will go out and buy your album. Brian Warner decided to act on his newly gained insight and created an alternate persona you may know as Marilyn Manson. He has, in my opinion, absolutely zero musical talent (although he did work with the übertalented producer Trent Reznor), but his lack of musical skill did not slow his career. By saying and doing insane things motivated solely by the desire to get under the skin of the evangelical establishment, he irritated Christians and caught the attention of these rock music seminars, going on to sell more than forty million albums. Not bad for a high school kid with little talent, huh? Christians got played.

As parents, we'd do well to pay attention, because this is a good lesson for us all to learn. Don't think I am suggesting that there shouldn't be rules; but when we are focused on the rules rather than the relationship, and we teach our kids to focus on the rules, we will start seeing what we should expect to happen: they will develop a deep desire to break the rules. And no matter how old we are, we all get a little buzz from rebellion.

A family in our congregation was recently given the remarkable gift of an Extreme Home Makeover from ABC. During that week, my brother Robbie and I worked with the cast and crew to see the project completed. We had so much fun on the set, and I even flew to Disney World to officiate and re-create the wedding of the couple's dreams. But for me, the most enjoyable moments included breaking the rules and sneaking in to see areas of the house where Ty and the gang were working, as if we were supposed to be there. We didn't have a pass to go into "off-limits" parts of the house, but we'd start saying stuff like, "Well, they need a 23-volt receptor up there," or "I've got to get up there and do some fire inspection" and would just walk right by like we knew what was going on. That little bit of rebellion feels good, right? It was fun. You know what I'm talking about. If you get an all-access pass to a concert only to find out that one section remains off-limits, you can either enjoy the show or focus on the single restriction given to you.

Real Christianity is about enjoying the show, which is the declaration of God's kingdom in ways both large and small. If you see the beauty around you, the fact that one area is off-limits does not concern you in the least. But if you let your mind spiral, the thoughts and questions about what may be hidden behind those doors will drive you crazy and you will miss the real party.

Righteousness as God's Restorative Justice

God's righteousness is powerful and multifaceted. We will spend much of this book exploring the fullness of its meaning. But we also know what his righteousness is not: a morality that can be attained by the works of man. The best simple translation of the word *righteousness* is "restorative justice." God is stepping into our brokenness and making things right, taking fragments shattered by sin and restoring them to fullness. The reality is that God is calling us to take part in his glory, which comes from heaven to earth, and to live in his abundance, together. Seeking his righteousness is about being an active agent for his restorative justice in all of creation.

What was and remains broken in this world because of the fall can be made whole. It can be set right. What does it look like for each of us to pull back and hear the words of Jesus anew? To view his actions and his life and ask, "How can I lean into a vibrant, true, and real faith that is not hyperfocused on rules and guidelines but on the kingdom of God?"

I believe the reason we are not living our lives in the light that real Christianity ignites is that we have ignored, distorted, and misunderstood the gospel according to Jesus. Join me on this journey through Scripture as we carefully attune our lives to the way of Jesus. Mark Batterson says it this way:

> The greatest risk is taking no risks. And it's not just risky, it's wrong. Righteousness is using all of our God-given gifts to their full God-given potential. Love doesn't play it safe; it takes risks. Love doesn't make excuses; it takes responsibility. Love doesn't see problems; it seizes opportunities to step up and step in. The Greek word for *strength* means "the antithesis of apathy." And Jesus is the ultimate example.[2]

May we emerge on the other side of these pages with a faith that calls us to action, believing that Jesus is making all things right and leading us to the land of promise.

My journey of faith has flourished for many reasons. I am blessed to be part of a family where Christianity has never been a stale ritual; it has led all of us to take radical steps of faith. I am also blessed to call many of the most inspiring and challenging voices in Christianity my dear friends. It is life changing to hear them speak at conferences and to read their books, but those interactions do not compare to the amazing conversations that we share over good food as we seek to be the church together. As we journey through *The Gospel According to Jesus*, I long for each of you to experience a taste of our table talk and eavesdrop on the insight that keeps me moving forward. It has been a great pleasure to visit with my friends and mentors about the content of this book. I hope that by inviting readers into my unique conversations with Gabe Lyons, Shane Claiborne, Rick McKinley, Alan Hirsch, Mark Batterson, and Dan Kimball, we will all see the gospel according to Jesus more clearly.

Interview with Gabe Lyons and Mark Batterson

My friend Gabe Lyons is the founder of "Q" and coauthor of *UnChristian*. He is a student of great ideas and a true believer that the church can reach its God-given potential. He and Mark Batterson (an author and pastor of National Community Church) share insight in this conversation that offers some practical ways to live out the gospel according to Jesus.

CHRIS: Gabe, in your book with David Kinnaman, *UnChristian*, you guys unveil some unsettling data about people's perceptions of the church. A lot of perceptions we hear from people are very similar to the perceptions would have about other religious establishments of Jesus' day and about the Pharisees, who were people who were basically more self-righteous than they were righteous. What has that journey been like, processing that information with the church and holding up a mirror to help us see ourselves for who we are?

GABE: Well, I think as we uncovered in *UnChristian*, the top perceptions of the church being judgmental, antihomosexual, sheltered, too political—when you start to look at the subtotal of these perceptions, a lot of them tend to find their basis in that one idea of the church as judgmental, which really comes from us having a higher view of ourselves than of other people. And for me the journey has been great to just recognize and to remember that moment when Christ saved me by grace, and to realize where I was at that point in time. I've realized that I'm no better than anybody else. No matter where I am on this journey, it's only through his grace that we even have the opportunity to come to that knowledge of him. When we start to think that it's something more than his grace that is making us righteous, we start to look at other people in one of the most ungodly ways we could, which is to see them as less than us. We see them as not equal to our standing and then project that onto them in how we treat them, how we talk about them, and how we interact or don't interact because we see them as less than how God sees us.

CHRIS: It's interesting to consider this historically, because we realize things don't change significantly through the centuries, do they? Martin Luther said that you can tell whether the church is rising or falling based on whether or not we understand justification—the acceptance that we're saved only by grace through faith—and that this grace is clearly a gift, one that is free and flows through Christ. So what do you think—are we, the church, rising or falling?

GABE: Well, there's certainly a strong enthusiasm among some Christians who I think have fully embraced God's grace in their lives. They understand and recognize that they're not perfect, but they also recognize that every moment they can avail themselves of Christ's power to work through them, amazing things are possible. They see God's love and signs of his kingdom showing up all over the place around them— in their vocations, in their work, in their art, in their music, in their entrepreneurial creations. They have a high view of Christ's power through them and a sober understanding of how limited they are at the human level to be able to really accomplish these significant things apart from his power.

And so they don't overdo or overthink their roles; they don't overemphasize their own power, although they appreciate it and know God's using it to advance his work, what he wants to do. So they don't have a small view of that, but they also realize they have a part to play in God's purposes to transform the world. They each recognize that the job is to be available, to sense where there's a need—to sense where something's broken and in need of restoration. Then they move toward those things or those people as God leads.

CHRIS: Mark, all of us here have grown up in traditions that focused on Jesus, but we also got a lot of legalism along the way. A lot of focus on what music we listen to and what words to say and having your hair a certain length or whatever—rules. The rules seemed to change over time, but the focus on the rules seemed to be fairly consistent. Talk to me about how focusing on *not* sinning doesn't necessarily help us not to sin. What does the gospel teach us about that? Mark, how do you think we guide our people through this paradox?

MARK: You know, the first thing that comes to mind is the conversation my wife and I had last night with our kids, who are hitting those preteen and early teen years. We've heard so many people say what you're saying, and I think it's so true. I think our parenting philosophy at this point is "keep them busy, keep them busy, keep them busy." Because if you don't, you're going to run into problems and they're going to get in trouble. I wonder if there's some correlation there with what we're talking about here.

If you focus on "don't sin, don't sin, don't sin," it's a double bind. It's like telling someone to be spontaneous. You can't do it once someone says to; it's almost like focusing on something you don't want will really bring it to fulfillment. So I'm a big believer (and this might be an overstatement) that 90 percent of our problems are not sin problems, but vision problems. We don't have enough God-given vision or God-ordained dreams. We don't have enough of those to keep us busy. And so we end up trying to keep ourselves busy with sin. I think that the vision piece is kind of the cure for some of the sins that we have. If you are keeping enough vision, then God is going to keep you busy with that. That's kind of my macro-philosophy. And it's why we as a church really focus on each member being a shareholder in our corporate vision; we also become a shareholder in each other's personal vision. (And, obviously, by *vision* I don't mean our own personal agenda for God, but the agenda he gives us.) I think shifting our focus toward that would go a long way toward solving some of this petty sinfulness that unnecessarily consumes us.

CHRIS: Beautifully said, brothers. That is an important word for all of us trying to parent our children well. I am so grateful to you both for your insight and love for the church.

TWO

Kingdom Without a King

*Without Jesus Christ man must be in vice and misery; with
Jesus Christ man is free from vice and misery; in Him is all our
virtue and all our happiness. Apart from Him there is but vice,
misery, darkness, death, despair.*

—Blaise Pascal

I am a sucker for stories of redemption. When I see a beach covered
in debris, a home obliterated by the earth's tremors, or a neighborhood of boarded-up apartments, I can see what it might become.
Redemption is never far away. Do you remember the first time you
saw *Extreme Makeover: Home Edition* on ABC? I'll never forget it.
I cried like a baby. If Jerry Lewis could get people this weepy, he
would have raised billions in his telethons. It may be formulaic, and
the crew of do-gooders may be better looking than anyone you will
ever meet in person, but when ABC drops into your community
to bless a family in your church with a brand-new home, it is a life-
changing experience to behold.

My friends, Larry and Melissa Beach, have centered their way of living on the teachings of Jesus. When they read that evidence of a pure faith is found in the ways that people care for "the least of these"—specifically orphans—they could not think of any excuses that might allow them to ignore this command. So they did something about it. Over the last fifteen years they have fostered more than eighty children in their home and enlarged their family by fifteen people through adoption.

When Hurricane Ike blew through Texas in 2008, its floodwaters wiped out their house. They moved their family into FEMA trailers, never missing a beat. When Ty Pennington brought a bullhorn to those trailers and knocked on the thin walls, it set off a chain of events that I never could have imagined. The story was so compelling that ABC extended the one-hour show to become a two-hour special that aired on Easter Sunday. The fruit of real Christianity rises to the top in every scene. My greatest joy was sharing the family's heart and love for Jesus with the cast and construction crew of volunteers that built this amazing new home. Everyone wanted to know why these people decided to serve children so selflessly. Why would someone adopt a child who is blind, deaf, brain damaged, and requires constant attention? Don't these children require specialists? What was this couple's motivation? There is no politically correct way to answer this question, but the answer is simple: Jesus.

Hundreds of great conversations sparked among the volunteers who built this house in one week's time. It was fascinating to see how many people were drawn to this experience because they longed to be part of someone getting his or her dream house. Volunteers would stop to reflect and imagine what it would be like to get their own dream houses. More than once I was able to say to someone basking in the grandeur of this new home, "No, the house itself isn't the dream for the Beach family. It is a big, beautiful home that accommodates their children with special needs, but the house is not the dream at all. The dream is what takes place in the house. In that house we see a declaration of the kingdom of God."

This family has humbly and simply said, "If you are among the least of these, if you're a child in need, one who would be otherwise institutionalized, then you're going to be part of our family. You're going to be brought here, not to an institution. You're going to be cared for and fed, you're going to have siblings, and you're going to share life with us." That's what we celebrate. The house could be gone in a minute—it wouldn't take much, right? One kid playing with matches is all it would take. It would be disappointing, but it would mean nothing. We would shed a few tears, but it's the declaration of the kingdom that is the most beautiful symbol in that house, no doubt about it.

When the whole project was completed, it included eight bedrooms, solar panels, an elevator, a therapy room, and much more, but the one thing that meant the most to Melissa Beach in this beautiful 6,340-square-foot home is the dining room table that will seat sixteen people—this whole family, plus one. Finally she would be able to eat a meal with her entire family. My guess is that we could cram twenty-five people around this big beautiful table if we tried hard. In the New Testament the table is a symbol of the kingdom, everybody coming together as equals, sharing food and grace in God's kingdom, at God's banqueting table. And it doesn't matter whether you're disabled; it doesn't matter what race or color or creed you are. We are all welcome; we are all children of God together at one table.

You may never get your dream house. Who cares? Will you declare the kingdom anyway? That is what truly matters. The kingdom that Jesus speaks of requires that we choose to pursue it. He says, "You can spend your life worrying and fretting about what you're going to wear, what you're going to drive, what you're going to live in, how you look to others, or," he goes on, "you can seek first the kingdom of God."[1] That which is here, that which is coming—God's reign on earth, where he is King and his kingdom is now—this kingdom is where grace abounds for all, where hope and healing are present.

It is interesting that Jesus offers this as an either/or situation and not a both/and situation. How much time do you spend worrying about physical needs, material possessions, bills, mortgages, tuition, and the like? Jesus says when we fret over such things, we are choosing the consumer way over the kingdom way (more to come on this in the next chapter). I don't know about you, but I am not the person that I am made to be when my focus is on the things of this world. I must leave behind one to fully embrace the other, and my true longing is not for more stuff; it is to be a citizen in a kingdom where poverty is eradicated, hope is restored, and forgiveness flows as freely as the air we breathe.

One week I was preaching at our church about the kingdom that is coming, and on the way out a young man grabbed me. He said, "Pastor, the kingdom is already here. Every Sunday I used to be in this same neighborhood (Montrose). I used to come down here to a bar called Emo's, and I'd start every night with a drop of ecstasy on my tongue and wash it down with Bacardi 151. That's what I did Sunday after Sunday. Now I come here instead, and I finish my evening with the body of Christ on my tongue and I wash it down with the blood of Christ. This is the kingdom of God." This man is experiencing the kingdom; he lives in its presence. We may not recognize it, we don't often see it, but it is right here, and we long to get past the mundane existence of religion and get a taste of the kingdom.

Heaven Can Come to Earth?

Over the last decade, the church has experienced a reawakening of kingdom theology. It is as if a lightbulb was turned on that illuminated the Gospels and Jesus' passionate teaching about his reign on earth as it is in heaven. We all want a taste of heaven here on earth, and a large part of the church has focused their attention on these images of kingdom life and pursued it with great vigor. If kingdom life is about the poor being fed, the thirsty quenched with clean water, and the sick being healed, then we should all devote our lives to these causes. At first this may sound right, good, and biblical. But make no mistake; a social gospel is no gospel at all. There can be no kingdom without the King!

I have seen the emptiness that comes with a human devotion to social activism, and it is even less appealing than the legalistic faith of my childhood. In a version of Christianity that focuses on the law and the rules, at least one has the chance to repeatedly encounter the Living Christ in the Scriptures. But a faith that is reduced to social service easily replaces the need for a Savior as we start to believe we can make it all work on our own. If the church is relegated to the ranks of a social service agency, even a highly effective agency, we have entirely missed our calling. My love for the poor will ebb and flow, and my commitment to do the right thing is fleeting. It is my response to the radical love and grace of Jesus the Liberating King that has the power to change the world. It is only when I live as one rescued that I see the source of salvation is not by the work of my own hands. A social gospel is not the gospel any more than a spiritual gospel is the gospel.

Some have defined the kingdom as a private, spiritual (read: Gnostic) domain. The belief is that God has come to save our individual souls and establish micro-kingdoms of his spiritual reign. This refusal to see God as a covenant God, who has set aside a people for himself to redeem all of creation, is a distortion of the gospel and, like the social gospel, in reality no gospel at all. There are no shortcuts to the kingdom of God; we must come together under the reign of the King. That is why the church is called out to journey together as we move toward the reign of God. It is always fascinating to hear the perspective of outsiders who visit our churches. We wonder if our sermons and worship reflect our actual beliefs, and through the eyes of strangers and critics we can evaluate our effectiveness in a new light.

A *Houston Chronicle* religion blogger and Unitarian pastor, Matt Tittle, recently came to visit Ecclesia, the church I pastor. He blogged about his experience and offered a unique point of view:

As I entered the converted warehouse at 2115 Taft St., I was comfortable. The gathering room to the worship space is a coffee shop and bookstore. A good coffee shop and bookstore run by the staff. . . . At Ecclesia, the focus was on the atmosphere and experience of worship. The most remarkable thing about Ecclesia was the age of the congregation. The average age was probably 27–29, with the mode (most common age) being a few years younger . . . Oh yeah, I forgot to mention the energy! One of my failsafe litmus tests for a vibrant, growing congregation is how noisy it is before and after the service. Noise is good. Ecclesia was noisy.

Where Ecclesia falls short, both for itself and for me, was its theology, which I describe as "salvation only through Christ." It was as I expected, but the emphasis on Jesus being the ONLY way not only doesn't speak to me, but doesn't speak to a growing number of Americans. Several recent religion research polls, including Barna and the Pew Forum, are indicating that American Christians are becoming more accepting of other paths to salvation. I think

Ecclesia would speak to even more people if they practiced and professed a more pluralistic theology and invitation to Jesus. I didn't take communion because the pastor said explicitly that at Ecclesia they believe that Jesus is the ONLY path to salvation. I believe that Jesus' teachings are a legitimate path, but not the only. It was at this point that I felt less welcome."[2]

There are many who examine the evils present in the church today and decide that Jesus may well be part of the problem and not the solution. If we embrace Jesus, are we rejecting many of his children who do not prefer a Messiah? Is declaring Jesus as the only path arrogant and dogmatic? If we look at our problems honestly, it becomes clear that we are not failing because we emulate Jesus too well; the problem is we look more like the religious establishment (Pharisees) than a reflection of Jesus. Matt Tittle offers some insight on many fronts that may help us diagnose the problem, but his remedy (less Jesus and more acceptance of the truth of all paths) is misguided and wide of the mark.

In Revelation 3, a particular church that is struggling to embrace its mission is offered insight from Jesus himself. Do you think this might apply to us as well?

Now pay attention; I am standing at the door and knocking. *Don't you hear?* If anyone hears My voice and opens the door, then I will come in to *visit with* you and to share a meal at your table, and you will be with Me. (v. 20)

Have you heard this passage before? I heard it often as I was growing up. In fact, it was given in the context of an invitation to salvation. There is a hymn that quotes the passage that we would sing often:

Softly and tenderly Jesus is calling,
Calling for you and for me;
See, on the portals He's waiting and watching,
Watching for you and for me.
Come home, come home,
Ye who are weary, come home;
Earnestly, tenderly, Jesus is calling,
Calling, O sinner, come home!"³

Basically, we were taught that Jesus was speaking to each of us individually, knocking on the door of our hearts. "It's me, Jesus; can I come in?" If you answered and opened the door, then Jesus would be present in your heart. But this passage was not written to you as an individual; actually, it's very, very clear—this is not even a *maybe*—it is clearly written to the whole church. So, imagine now our Messiah knocking on the door of his church as you go back and reread Revelation 3:20. Do you hear the difference when you listen as part of God's people rather than an individual follower? The gospel according to Jesus is very clear. There is no "me-and-Jesus" kind of relationship—each of us becomes part of one very large family.

Imagine it this way: Let's say you and I were becoming friends, so one day you say, "Hey Chris, you like baseball and I like a baseball. Let's get together often, eat étouffée, and catch a baseball game." (And, for the record, if you didn't mind having Mexican food before games from time to time, and if you were not a Cubs fan, we would likely become fast friends.) But then one day you drop a bomb on me. "Hey, Chris. Just to be clear, I really love hanging out with you. Your family, though, kind of annoys me. Your wife is bossy, your kids whine, and your brother smacks his food when he eats. And, I do want to be your friend, but please keep them away from me." What would happen next is that we would fight—I would punch you; you would not be my friend. It would not go well. But do you see the correlation?

You can't say to Jesus, "Hey, Jesus, you and I have this great intimate personal relationship, but I am just not into your people. They are too much work. Very needy. They don't keep their word and they wear too much makeup." Well, you would be right on some fronts. Jesus' people are not perfect. They are broken, they will disappoint you, but they will also inspire you. They will fail you, but they will also love you. If you love Jesus and want to be part of Jesus' reign, it also means that you are part of Jesus' (broken) people. Welcome to the family.

The Mark of a Jesus Church

Revelation is not some mysterious book that you need a DaVinci pinwheel to decode. You don't have to chart it out with an apocalyptic calendar shaped like a lion that counts down the days to the rapture. That is not what the book is about. It's a book written to churches being persecuted. They are suffering, they are being oppressed by Rome, they need hope, and they find it in the person of Jesus. That's the clear message of Revelation: you need hope, and Jesus is your hope. So if you're suffering, if you are going through hard times, if you are looking for hope, Revelation is a great book to read. It is a book written to the church to focus them on Jesus and offer them an undying hope.

> Let the person who is able to hear, listen to *and follow* what the Spirit proclaims to all the churches. Write *down My words and send them* to the messenger of the church in Laodicea. "These are the words of the Amen, the Faithful and True Witness, the Beginning of God's creation: I know your works." (3:13–15)

Can you hear these words just as if Jesus were speaking directly to your church? Jesus is really clear: Show me your faith that works. It's not about the works themselves, but about the active, living faith that's being, creating, and re-creating.

> I know your works. You are neither cold *with apathy* nor hot *with passion*. It would be better if you were one or the other. *But you are neither*. So, because you are lukewarm, neither cold nor hot, I will vomit you out of My mouth. You claim: 'I am rich, I have accumulated riches, and I need nothing.' But you do not realize that you are miserable, pathetic, poor, blind, and naked. (vv. 15–17)

This is interesting; here Jesus states the mark of a good church: a church that realizes we are miserable, pathetic, poor, blind, and naked. My church will never likely have commercials or billboards, but if we did, it should likely declare something like:

> *Come to Ecclesia.*
> *We are miserable, pathetic, poor, blind, and naked.*

And God is using us. May we never think more of ourselves than this.

The passage in Revelation continues:

> So here is what I suggest you do: buy *true gold* from Me (gold refined by fire so that you can be *truly* rich), white garments (to cover you so that you can keep the shame of your nakedness from showing), and eye ointment (to treat your eyes so that you may see clearly). Those I love I also correct and discipline. (vv. 18–19)

How many of us struggle with God's correction and discipline? When we come to God as confessional people, we begin to hear words from the Spirit: "Hey, that thing you were up to this week . . . remember your impatience? Your anger? It is not of me." God deals very specifically with each of our hearts and actions. Know that this is a voice of love, not a voice of condemnation; don't be confused. There is someone who condemns, and that is the adversary. God, through his Spirit, will guide and correct each of us as a loving parent. "Those that I love, I correct." As parents, we daily encourage our kids in this way too: "I'm correcting you because I love you, because I want to see you grow in the right direction. I am your biggest fan. I want to keep showing you the path." What if our kids grew up to be Cubs fans or something? We can't let that happen; we have to be on top of it.

Once he has corrected us, God says, "Therefore, be shamelessly committed *to Me* and turn back [literally, *repent*]." Following Jesus our King cannot be boiled down to some religious rituals where we come, sit, sing some songs, throw a few dollars in the offering plate, and leave professing a Christian life. We cannot be Sunday Christians. If that's what you are doing, just stop. Do something else.

The shameless pursuit of Jesus as King and his reign in our lives will begin to change everything. "Now pay attention; I am standing at the door and knocking" (Rev. 3:20). He's knocking at our churches today just as surely as he stood rapping upon the church doors in Laodicea, saying, "I would like to come in. You have written My name on the building, but I am not welcomed through the door! You're not up to My things in the world" Brothers and sisters, there can be nothing worse than Jesus knocking at the door while we are so busy with our own agenda that we can't hear him. Every area of our lives must recalibrate around the work of Jesus.

My younger brother, Robbie, who leads worship at Ecclesia, has a friend who attended an art show called The Starving Artist at our church gallery, Ex Nihilo. The art show was an exhibition of some great art from two homeless brothers in our church. This friend of Robbie's serves a big Presbyterian church somewhere, a good church. He said, "This is so different for me, because I wonder if homeless people would even feel very welcome or comfortable in our church. In your church they're like rock stars; they are fabulous artists loved by the entire church." Do you ever wonder about the outcasts in your city? They might be the superstars to Jesus:

I am standing at the door and knocking. *Don't you hear?* If anyone hears My voice and opens the door, then I will come in to *visit with* you and to share a meal at your table, and you will be with Me. (Rev. 3:20)

This is the familiar metaphor from the Scriptures, one of dining together, one of celebration of his grace and his goodness.

The one who conquers *through faithfulness even unto death* I will place next to Me on My throne, just as I Myself conquered and took a place *of honor* with My Father on His throne. Let the person who is able to hear, listen to *and follow* what the Spirit proclaims to all the churches. (Rev. 3:21–22)

May this be true of us, fellow called-out ones.

Say My Name

As we hear Jesus speak, we are changed. Our journeys may be similar in many ways to the triumphs and struggles experienced by the disciples. If you read and follow Peter's conversations with Jesus, you may see what the two of you have in common. May we hear and respond to the voice and the truth of Jesus:

> Jesus then went to Caesarea Philippi.
>
> Jesus (to His disciples): Who do people say the Son of Man is?
>
> Disciples: Some say John who ritually cleanses people.[4] And some say Elijah. And some say Jeremiah or one of the other prophets.
>
> Jesus: And you? Who do you say that I am?
>
> Simon Peter: You are the Liberating King. You are the Son of the living God. (Matt. 16:13–16)

I say this often at my church, and I say it again here: the "Christ" title is not Jesus' last name. It's a declaration that he is the King, a King who came to free us and to liberate us from the bondage of sin and slavery. And in doing so, he is making all things right in this world, restoring the Garden he created.

> Jesus: Simon, son of Jonah, your knowledge is a mark of blessing. For you didn't learn this truth from your friends or from teachers or from sages you've met on the way. You learned it from My Father in heaven. This is why I have called you Peter (rock): for on this rock I will build My church." (vv. 17–18)

Wow. When Jesus gives you a name, that's a pretty big deal, right? You've been Cephas your whole life, and then one day after being bold enough to speak the truth, Jesus gives you a brand-new name. It could have been anything! It could have been more hippie, like Moondust or Spring Breeze or Flower of the Meadow . . . you never know. But Peter gets a strong name—Rock, like a wrestler. It means he's going to appear in many feature films with very poor acting skills (joke). This is a good name, so you can imagine the expression on Peter's face, right? Maybe he sat up straighter. He's got to be feeling pretty sure of himself right now. "Yeah, I'm Rock! Okay, I'll take that. I'll be Rock. Solid." It's certainly a boost. He answered faithfully and he got it.

> The church will reign triumphant even at the gates of hell. Peter, I give you the keys to the kingdom of heaven. Whatever you bind on earth will be bound in heaven, and whatever you loose on earth will be loosed in heaven. (vv. 18–19)

Then Jesus' tone changes:

> And Jesus ordered His disciples *to keep these teachings secret.*
> Jesus: You must tell no one that I am the Liberator.
>
> Then Jesus began to tell the disciples *about what would happen to Him. He said* He would have to go to Jerusalem, and there the elders, chief priests, and scribes would meet Him; He would suffer at their hands, and He would be killed. But three days later, He would be raised *to new life.*
>
> *As Jesus spoke of the things to come,* Peter took Him aside. *Sad and confused, and maybe a little bit prideful,* Peter chastised Jesus.
> Peter: No, Lord! Never! These things that You are saying—they will never happen to You!
> Jesus (*turning to Peter*): Get away from Me, Satan! (vv. 20–23)

Now comparing these two passages of Jesus' interactions with Peter—one minute he's the Rock with the right answers, and the next minute he's Satan—I imagine Peter did one of those classic double takes, eyes bulging in disbelief. "Satan? What? I am Rock, Jesus, remember? I am solid." The truth is, Peter is like most of us on his spiritual journey—he takes two steps forward and one step back. We fail. We get it right and then we get it wrong, and all the while God is redeeming us through a continual progression. But there's no instant perfection. It just won't happen this side of heaven. On this side of heaven, we simply continue to pursue Jesus.

Ultimately Jesus says, "Peter, you missed it. You're wrong. But I continue to love you. I'll deal with you and I'll lead you along the way." We should find great encouragement in the life of Peter because he gets it right again later on. Then he denies Jesus. Then he has a realization. Then he really gets the church going. He could be any of us.

This is the beauty God has called us to participate in. Not a life of perfection but a journey. One that will send us all the way to the gates of hell and allow us to see God redeem all things and make all things right. This is not a stale, mind-numbing religious existence. This is a quest into the depths of darkness to shine the light of life and join God's transforming work in this beautifully broken world.

PRAYER

Lord, we acknowledge that we are often like Peter, one moment experiencing a spiritual breakthrough and the next falling on our faces. We are so grateful that your grace is not created by our faithfulness, but by yours. Would you guide us toward the brokenness in our lives, neighborhoods, and the slums that litter the globe with a faith that believes redemption is coming? Give us eyes to see the work of our King and follow faithfully. Amen.

Interview with Rick McKinley, Dan Kimball, and Shane Claiborne of Vintage Faith Church

Long before Rick McKinley, Shane Claiborne, and Dan Kimball were writing books, they were just my friends who demonstrated the kind of passion for God and neighbor that inspired me. Over the decades these are the people I seek out when I am discouraged. Their lives and stories never fail to urge me to get back in the game and believe that God is in control of the ultimate outcomes.

CHRIS: Rick, you explained so well in our last conversation the struggle to embrace individuality rather than relationality. As we attempt to leave behind religious rigor and the false substitute of righteousness, and begin to live in that unison with the Trinity (we both know this experientially; we're seeing this in the data from Barna), we see clearly that for so many

Christians, that's what faith has become—this ritual to live by the rules. What do you think are the ramifications when we begin to live in that relational unity with the Trinity? How does that play out? What looks different about church?

RICK: I think there are a lot of characteristics. One would be individualism. What you see is this big movement away from the larger organization and people wanting to go into smaller community pockets to live out the "one-anothers." And yet, those will completely implode because it's really not about a big church organization or about the small communal church. It's actually that what's going on within the Trinity is something that is now going on within me, and now I will go and express it within the context of community. So all the "one-anothers" in the New Testament are just simply descriptions of what's going on within the Godhead. Does that make sense?

CHRIS: Yes. Perfect sense. If we are to understand that we are created in the image of God, a primary part of that understanding must be that relationality saturates everything. If God is triune, then God is in a constant state of relationship. When we begin to understand ourselves as merely an individual, we are violating the essence of the *imago dei*.

RICK: When I'm caught up in Christ, I'm experiencing a relationship with him; therefore I can devote myself to you, I can serve you, because it's Christ in me. But I think we spend so much time on how we structure our churches, thinking that "some new form" will actually answer the ontological problem, which is, "I'm not living out of the center of being united with Christ." And yet, if I live out of that center, I don't think forms are that important because it changes the motive for everything I do.

So I can come into a mega church and worship Christ and let the love of Christ for the Father overflow through me to the Father. I can go to a small group Bible study and love those people, and Christ will pour himself out there too. We spend so much time on structures and forms rather than going deep into the biblical theology of this kind of Trinitarian union. This union changes how we live with one another, and it clearly changes how we understand mission.

Chris, you and I go to churches where our people are really "busy" for Jesus. They want to go work for the kingdom. Other churches say their people don't move, that they just want to study the Bible. But both can find themselves ending up in sin. I might be all stuck in social justice, yet I don't like Jesus. But I want to say that what I am doing is for the kingdom. But how can the kingdom show up if the King is not around?

CHRIS: Well, it's exactly what you are saying. It is hard to explain, and that's part of why it has to be incarnate. That's what Jesus said: let me speak the truth for you, and let me demonstrate that I am the truth. Dan, you often talk about the importance of relationality in our theology, carrying over to the way we do evangelism and discipleship. What does that look like at your church, Vintage Faith?

DAN: As we live life together, questions eventually come up with people, like, "So you really believe he rose from the dead?" And I say, "Yes, I do." These pragmatic, real-life questions come up. "So you would believe God's best for me would not be living and sleeping with my girlfriend here . . ." And although that's not the focus of the conversation on what it means to know Jesus, all of a sudden these things come up. The good part is that before, these conversations may have never come to fruition because people didn't trust the church and had so many wacky impressions; now they come up and talk.

CHRIS: Yeah, we must realize the King has got to be present. That's the part of what the whole thing is about. We want the kingdom, but we can't live without the King.

DAN: I recently went to the Presbyterian Church USA meeting, and I don't know if the name Jesus even came up once (at least for the hour I sat in there it didn't), but it was all about having the food pantry and "Here is the picture of the closet," partnering with this or that downtown association. But there was no sense that this is rooted in faith in Jesus. That becomes self-righteousness.

CHRIS: Yeah, more works-based. It's no longer by grace through faith in Jesus. No matter what the works are, they promote self-righteousness rather than the righteousness of Christ. So it's just this endless circle of going mad, and our sinful nature wants to lead us away from this true gospel.

DAN. Right. Here's an example. Last Friday we had three bands at our church. This young, twenty-three-year-old leading it raised a thousand dollars for Haiti, and they had seven or eight Compassion International kids that were also sponsored that night. There wasn't a mandatory "make sure this happens" in regards to raising money or sponsoring kids. It just happened naturally. It's the culture. And I can tell you this, the guy that put it on is very passionate about seeing people put faith in Jesus and follow him. It was cool hearing about that.

CHRIS: Yes, for both of us these are the greatest joys of being a pastor. It's observing the faith that bears fruit that we hear James talking about. We are not working to create things, but we are working because faith leads us to that path. It's out of pure response. Faith is a total gift, but we see people naturally responding; it is so different than legalism and so freeing.

Shane, you approach this from a different place. How would you describe this tension between seeking the King and kingdom? When was the discovery for you to see more clearly what the kingdom of God is about?

SHANE: I think it was when I realized that you can worship Jesus without following him. The Scriptures (in Amos and the prophets and others) talk about how we can sing songs and burn incense, but if justice doesn't roll out to the poor and oppressed, then it's just stench in God's nose and noise in God's ears. James's true religion cares for the widows and the orphans. When I started reading these things, it started to make a lot of sense for me in light of Jesus—that he's not just offering us a presentation of ideas but an invitation to join a movement that's about embodying God's love and justice and about bringing it down on earth and not just promising people life after death, but that it begins right now.

CHRIS: So true. It is a movement, bound in relationship, that seeks to transform the world. Sounds like good news to me.

THREE

What Is the Gospel?

*Avoid a sugared gospel as you would shun sugar of lead. Seek
the gospel which rips up and tears and cuts and wounds and
hacks and even kills, for that is the gospel that makes alive
again. And when you have found it, give good heed to it. Let it
enter into your inmost being. As the rain soaks into the ground,
so pray the Lord to let his gospel soak into your soul.*

–Charles Spurgeon

In my experience, we learn best when we engage in rich, thoughtful conversations that explore the great tensions of life and faith. I
enjoy conversations about diverse topics, not just theology. If you
work on an offshore rig, I want to hear all about it. I am mesmerized
by the ways that you are able keep that floating mechanism func-
tioning. The mysterious creative journey that every artist travels is
intriguing to me; please tell me more. I love finding and discussing
spiritual themes in unlikely places because, ultimately, these conversations always lead back to the life, teachings, and actions of Jesus.

These interactions are more significant than they may appear on the surface, for whenever we explore a subject, we find truth and insight in totally unexpected ways. I find that, while searching for deep truths in conversations about a unique vocation, scientific theory, creative process, movie, or TV series, questions surface that expose our understanding of truth. We're then afforded the opportunity to see how our paradigms align with the gospel as told through the actions of Jesus. Even now you are probably wondering how your job or hobby grafts into the teaching of Jesus, but I assure you, it does. If you seek truth well, you will find rudiments of explicit Christian truth, and you will likely find yourself saying, "Wow. These ideas resonate with the gospel, although they are not exactly the gospel." So how do we engage a world of ideas, truth, lies, and half-truths while seeking out the whole truth? We allow the Scriptures to be the standard by which everything is compared.

I enjoy writing about faith and popular culture. My friend, Greg Garrett, and I spent a year researching the palpable and obscure references to faith in the Messianic blockbuster *The Matrix*. My most recent obsession is the ABC hit show *Lost*; it is filled with biblical allusions, references to philosophy, and a healthy dose of the human condition. As you discuss the latest episode of your favorite show, you will probably find that the door is continually open to delving deeper into the gospel. But pop culture is fallible and will not lead you to truth on its own—one must watch these shows with a prayerful heart and the Bible in one hand. In the three *Matrix* films and in *Lost*, you get to uncover all kinds of spiritual truths and nuggets that are hidden here and there; but when you are reading through the Bible, you don't have to mine for it. Truth is not hidden anywhere; it's an open treasure chest in your hands. You may need to wrestle with the parables of Jesus and seek some historical context for the letters of Paul, but the gospel clearly shines through the Bible. It is not an exasperating puzzle that requires assembly.

So what deep truths do the Scriptures give us? How do they guide us, and what is the central message of the gospel? There is a sense of accepted Christian belief and practice that many in the church could articulate quite easily, but is it the gospel? Are you able to articulate the gospel according to Jesus? If not, you must take some time to shore up your understanding of the gospel before you endeavor to explore any currents of gospel message running in popular culture.

I'm prone to hyperboles. In the passion of preaching, I will often make bold declarations (read: exaggerations) that the current Sunday's text is "my favorite in all of the Bible," only to give the same honor to another passage the following week. I am not lying; I just fall in love with the passage of Scripture that God is using to speak to me at that moment. But I want to be clear—I am not overstating my case when I tell you that the question we are wrestling with in this chapter is the most important question followers of Jesus the Liberating King can ever ask themselves: what is the gospel?

The Gospel of Truth

I could probably pull a Jay Leno and set up a microphone on the street and ask people to share their thoughts about the gospel at random. I hope many people would mention the essentials. I think, for the most part, a majority would admit, "I need to think about that question," or "I'm not really sure. I don't know that I could articulate it." Or often what happens is we start our explanation by talking about salvation, but salvation isn't the gospel. Salvation is the *result* of the gospel. Others might tell personal accounts or give an individualized picture of the gospel, which is not the gospel either. The gospel preached in the Bible is a kingdom for all people—it is not a modern, individualistic experience.

I want you to consider some of the best definitions of the gospel offered to us by theologians and church leaders. Once we have delved deep into the best articulations of the gospel, as well as Paul's definition in Romans, I will ask you to write out your own and commit it to memory. This journey is about understanding the gospel in our hearts and heads so it can lead us to a natural and heartfelt enunciation we can express with our mouths.

Lesslie Newbigin has helped shape my understanding of the gospel more than anyone else outside the biblical canon. Lesslie was a missionary to India in a day when most people were not doing missions very well; some were literally shipping over pipe organs and choir robes and teaching indigenous people to act like white folks. It was sinful and wrong, really. What Lesslie did was different. He began to ask, "What if the gospel is supposed to dwell in this culture in a unique and beautiful way that's very distinctly Indian?" He was a brilliant man who offered many gifts to the world, and although I never met him, I consider him a mentor. Newbigin says,

> I think we've used the word gospel without giving as much attention as we need to the question of what actually we mean by that word. We don't mean Christianity. Christianity is what generations of us have made of the gospel and we know we have often made a mess of it . . . The specific responsibility which has been given to the church and to nobody else is the responsibility to bear witness to the reality of Jesus' victory.[1]

That's a focus of the gospel: we step into the places of darkness because we believe that through Jesus we will be victorious.

Newbigin goes on: "The announcing of the good news about the Kingdom is empty verbiage if there is nothing happening to make the news credible."[2]

This is important. Jesus summarizes it very simply, right? He said, "I speak the truth, and I am the truth." But the truth must be embodied and seen in a living way. This is what the gospel is and what the church is called to do: to be the hands and feet of Christ, living out truth in a tangible and transformative way.

Evangelion is the Greek word that we translate as "gospel" or "good news." If your take on the gospel does not sound like good news, it is not the gospel. Pope Benedict XVI offers a very good summary of some of the historical implications of the word *evangelion*. He says:

The term has recently been translated as "good news." That sounds attractive, but it falls far short of the order of magnitude of what is actually meant by the word *evangelion*. This term figures in the vocabulary of the Roman emperors, who understood themselves as lords, saviors, and redeemers of the world . . . The idea was that what comes from the emperor is a saving message, that it is not just a piece of news, but also a changing of the world for the better. When the Evangelists adopt this word, and it thereby becomes the generic name for their writings, what they mean to tell us is this: What the emperors, who pretend to be gods, illegitimately claim, really occurs here—a message endowed with plenary authority, a message that is not just talk but reality . . . The Gospel is not just informative speech, but performative speech—not just the imparting of information, but action, efficacious power that enters into the world to save and transform. Mark speaks of the "gospel of God," the point being that it is not the emperors who can save the world, but God. And it is here that God's word, which is at once word and deed, appears; it is here that what the emperors merely assert, but cannot actually perform, truly takes place. For here it is the real Lord of the world—the Living God—who goes into action.[3]

Our good news is radically different from the empty declarations of the Roman emperors; it is not merely an announcement that offers important information, it leads us to an action: redemption. A theologian named William Tyndale said this of the gospel:

Evangelion (that we call the gospel) is a Greek word and signifieth good, merry, glad and joyful tidings, that maketh a man's heart glad and maketh him sing, dance, and leap for joy . . . [This gospel is] all of Christ the right David, how that he hath fought with sin, with death, and the devil, and overcome them: whereby all men that were in bondage to sin, wounded with death, overcome of the devil are without their own merits or deservings loosed, justified, restored to life and saved, brought to liberty and reconciled unto the favor of God and set at one with him again: which tidings as many as believe laud, praise and thank God, are glad, sing and dance for joy.[4]

We all need to hear this clearly. There won't be a definition of the gospel that's nearly adequate if it is not centered in Jesus the King who liberates. It was a declaration that Jesus *is* King, and Tyndale explains this in a beautiful way. This good news ought to make you leap and dance. One of the indicators of how well we grasp and live out the gospel is our "leaping and dancing." Does your church celebrate well? Are you a festive crew, or might some describe you as gloomy? As people of the good news, we will not always be cheery, but we must live as those who know, in the midst of our struggles with sin and death, that we are victorious through Christ.

I have a friend, Andy, who is pretty creative, and a little straight-laced. But now he has a really beautiful girlfriend and suddenly he is learning to salsa dance. He is not a guy you would envision becoming a salsa dancer, but a beautiful woman has inspired him. What she doesn't know is that, like me, any guy pursuing a woman will say things like, "Yeah, I totally love to dance salsa," and then as soon as they're married it will never happen again. Things start coming up. "My back hurts. I'm not feeling like salsa dancing is a good idea today . . ." But for now Andy is dedicated to winning this girl, and he's experiencing the kind of joy that the Lord gives us, the kind that would lead you, even if you were not a dancer, to dance.

D. A. Carson explains it this way: "The gospel is integrally tied to the Bible's story line. Indeed, it is incomprehensible without understanding that story line."[5] This is part of the mistake that Christians make too often: we try to explain the gospel by extracting a few truths, facts, or propositions from the story. The church I grew up in loved to produce these little tracts that we would hand out or leave for a waiter instead of a monetary tip at restaurants. (If you have ever been a waiter, you know what I am talking about. God bless our beautiful brothers and sisters who thought this was a really loving idea.) So they produced this one tract about Romans, what I believe to be the most complex, beautiful, and profound book in the Bible, and called it "The Roman Road." It was the book of Romans summarized in four statements. Four sentences. That is impossible; you lose the entire narrative! D. A. Carson says without that narrative, without that story line, the gospel is incomprehensible. Carson's definition of the gospel is lengthy because it includes some good storytelling:

> God is the sovereign, transcendent and personal God who has made the universe, including us, his image-bearers. Our misery lies in our rebellion, our alienation from God, which, despite his forbearance,

attracts his implacable wrath. But God, precisely because love is of the very essence of his character, takes the initiative and prepared for the coming of his own Son by raising up a people who, by covenantal stipulations, temple worship, systems of sacrifice and of priesthood, by kings and by prophets, are taught something of what God is planning and what he expects. In the fullness of time his Son comes and takes on human nature. He comes not, in the first instance, to judge but to save: he dies the death of his people, rises from the grave and, in returning to his heavenly Father, bequeaths the Holy Spirit as the down payment and guarantee of the ultimate gift he has secured for them—an eternity of bliss in the presence of God himself, in a new heaven and a new earth, the home of righteousness. The only alternative is to be shut out from the presence of this God forever, in the torments of hell. What men and women must do, before it is too late, is repent and trust Christ; the alternative is to disobey the gospel.[6]

Tim Keller, a friend who pastors a church called Redeemer Presbyterian in New York City, puts it this way:

The "gospel" is the good news that through Christ the power of God's kingdom has entered history to renew the whole world. When we believe and rely on Jesus' work and record (rather than ours) for our relationship to God, that kingdom power comes upon us and begins to work through us. Through the person and work of Jesus Christ, God fully accomplishes salvation for us, rescuing us from judgment for sin into fellowship with him, and then restores the creation in which we can enjoy our new life together with him forever.[7]

My dear friend Rick McKinley, who pastors Imago Dei Church in Portland, Oregon, lays out the gospel in his book, *This Beautiful Mess*:

Sometimes it seems as though we find two gospels in the New Testament—the gospel of Jesus and the gospel about Jesus. The gospel of Jesus is usually taken to mean His announcement of the kingdom and the life He embodied in His loving actions toward the world. The gospel about Jesus refers to his atoning work on the cross and His resurrection, through which we can receive the forgiveness of sin through our faith and repentance. I believe, however, that the two are actually one gospel and that when we lose the tension that comes from holding both together, we experience an unhealthy and unbiblical pendulum swing in our faith. If all we value is the salvation gospel, we tend to miss the rest of Christ's message. Taken out of context of the kingdom, the call to faith in Christ gets reduced to something less than what the New Testament teaches. The reverse is also true: if we value a kingdom gospel at the expense of the liberating message of the Cross and the empty tomb and a call to repentance, we miss a central tenet of kingdom life. Without faith in Jesus, there is no transferring of our lives into the new world of the kingdom.[8]

Are you still with me? This is all so very important. Can you see your own definition of the good news taking shape? Let me offer you my articulation and the one shared with us by Martin Luther and the apostle Paul. Here's a definition I shaped to explain the gospel (in my own words):

The gospel is the good news that God is calling out all people to be redeemed by the power residing in the life, death, and ultimate resurrection of Jesus the Liberating King. These "called-out ones" are rescued from a life of slavery, sin, and failure to become emissaries in a new kingdom set to join the redemption of the entire creation, groaning and longing to be redeemed.

Last year I had the privilege of going to Germany and experiencing a kind of theological tour. Some friends and I spent time in the pubs where Martin Luther spent his life talking about the gospel. My life isn't always good, but that particular week it soared. We slept in a hotel adjacent to Luther's home and contemplated his deep commitment to Christ and the church. During those days, devouring bratwurst, I deeply pondered Luther's definition of the gospel:

> For at its briefest, the gospel is a discourse about Christ, that he is the Son of God and became man for us, that he died and was raised, and that he has been established as Lord over all things. This much St. Paul takes in hand and spins out in his epistles. He bypasses all the miracles and incidents [in Christ's ministry] which are set forth in the four Gospels, yet he includes the whole gospel adequately and abundantly. This may be seen clearly and well in his greeting to the Romans.[9]

If you're unfamiliar with the book of Romans, let me tell you what makes it distinct and different. It is very different from all the other writings of Paul in the New Testament, which were personal letters to people he knew well. In Paul's other letters he catches up with his community. "Hey, how's so-and-so? Who's been sick? How are you doing? Are you all still following the teaching I last shared with you? Listen, quit getting drunk when you take communion. Sleep with only your spouses." Paul has a rapport with these friends, and because of that, he could joke with them, rebuke them, and express his affection for them.

The people he wrote to in Corinth, Philippi, Ephesus, and the like had heard Paul preach over and over. In fact, there is a story in Acts where Paul is preaching a very long sermon, so long that one of the kids sitting in a windowsill dozes off and falls out of the second-story window. (We pastors find some comfort in knowing that people also fell asleep during the sermons of the apostle Paul.) Whenever Paul was coming to town, you'd probably hear conversations like, "Did you hear that Paul's coming to town? He's probably going to preach on the gospel of good news again. Yes, I bet he reminds us about forgiveness of sin and struggling with sin and what redemption looks like in Jesus the Liberating King. We can be sure he will talk a lot about Jesus. He's definitely going to tell that story again where he met Jesus and there was a bright light and he fell down . . . We love that one. It's a big hit. Have you heard his Pharisee jokes? Those are good." But the people Paul is writing to in Rome hadn't heard those sermons—Paul had never even been to Rome. He kept planning to go there, but he just couldn't ever make it. So the book of Romans became kind of like Paul's "greatest hits," where he is writing out what he would have preached had he been able to get to Rome. How do you start a letter like that? With the gospel. So here is Paul, laying out the gospel in Romans 1:

> Paul, a servant of Jesus the Liberating King, called by God to be His emissary [literally, *apostle*] and appointed to tell the good news of the things promised long ago by God, spoken by prophets, and recorded in the Holy Scriptures. All of this good news is about His Son: who was (from a human perspective) born of David's royal line *and ultimately* designated to be the *true* Son of God with power upon His resurrection from death by the Spirit of holiness. I am speaking of Jesus the Liberating King, our Lord.
>
> *And, here's what He's done:* He has graced us and sanctioned us as His emissaries [literally, apostles] whose mission is to spread the *one true and* obedient faith to all people in the name of Jesus. (vv. 1–5)

Who? All of us—God's emissaries. Paul has articulated our life mission for us, and yet we're still kind of going, "Are you sure he's talking about *us*?" He goes on and makes it clear: "This includes you: you too have been called by Jesus the Liberating King" (v. 6). All of us—the ecclesia, the church—are called as emissaries. To our modern-day ears *emissary* sounds a bit like a governmental kind of position; maybe a cabinet-level position, a diplomat. A diplomat would be the kind of person who goes around and talks about things. (It's actually my dream job. I'm praying one day a new president will call me and say, "Chris, would you like to be the diplomat to the Bahamas?" Of course, I would have to pray and consider it, but could see myself saying yes to that position.) To us, being an emissary is like being a diplomat or a politician, and in our culture, politicians often seem like people who don't actually do anything. They talk about things, they write up bills, but they're not out there getting their hands dirty. But the sort of emissary that Paul speaks of is more like a Peace Corps volunteer. They see what's broken and they get their hands dirty fixing it.

If Jesus calls you, if you have a relationship with Christ, you have an office as an emissary. Many come to my church, Ecclesia Houston, and believe that I and other leaders at the church can do this kind of work because we are "professional Christians"—that we're the ones that really go and get things done and the most everyone else can do is just come and learn a few things and throw a buck or two in the offering plate on the way out. But that's a lie from the pit of hell. There is not a more dangerous lie that exists in the church. Your calling is equal to and as important as my calling. There is no difference. We are *all* called to be the hands and feet of Christ, to radically change the world. It begins with our lives and our hearts as we experience God's redemption near and far. Until we begin to catch on to that, we will be missing something beautiful and important.

Paul says,

> To all those who are God's beloved saints in Rome:
>
> May grace and peace from God our Father and the Lord Jesus, the Liberating King, surround you.
>
> First, I thank my God through the Liberator, Jesus, for all of you because *we are joined by faith as family, and* your faith is spreading across the world. *Because of your influence, many are becoming aware of our Savior.* (Rom. 1:7–8)

Part of our work as the church is sharing the contagious nature of faith. People should come through our communities saying, "You guys are nice. You actually like each other and you're not some crazy institution that fights over things. If this is what Christianity is like, I think that I want in after all." Is your faith contagious? This is what the people in Rome were doing. It was catching on. Other people were noticing. Thrilled with the Roman Christians, Paul says,

> For *I call* God as my witness—whom I worship in the spirit and serve in making known the gospel—He alone knows how often I mention you in my prayers. I find myself constantly praying for you and hoping it's in God's will for me to be with you soon. I desperately want to see you so that I can share some gift of the Spirit to strengthen you. Plus, I know that when we come together *something beautiful will happen* as we are encouraged by each other's faith. (vv. 9–12)

Can you hear Paul sharing one of the greatest struggles in his life? He talks about it in other places, too, but many of the churches were getting a bit greedy about his time, perhaps complaining, "Hey, Paul, you hadn't come to see us in a while, and then you went over there to Corinth. And when you got out of jail, you should have come here and, well, we're mad. We want more Paul." And Paul simply said, "I can't be everywhere. I'm not Jesus. I'm not omnipresent. I can only be in one place at one time." This is one struggle I can relate to as a pastor. It reminds me why we do not follow a man or woman. If there is anyone who comes to mind as you are reading this that you feel you pull on too much, define yourself by, or grumble about if you do not get his or her time or attention, try praying for him or her instead. Show a little kindness; it goes a long way.

> If, my brothers and sisters, you did not already know, my plans were set to meet you *in Rome*, but time and circumstances have forced every trip to be cancelled until now. I have deeply desired to see some good fruit among you just as I have seen with so many non-Jewish believers. *You see,* I am in *tremendous* debt to those of various nationalities, from non-Jews to barbarians, from the wisest of the wise to the idle wanderer. So you can imagine how eager I am to join you and to teach the good news in *the mighty and diverse city* of Rome. (vv. 13–15)

And here comes my favorite part. As you read these words from Paul, you will begin to sit up in your chair. You'll begin to feel a kind of a gospel adrenaline that whispers to you, "You were made to stand in this kind of adversity. This is who you're called to be."

> For I am not *the least bit* embarrassed about the gospel. *I won't shy away from it,* because it is God's power to save every person who believes: first the Jew, and then the non-Jew. You see, in the good news, God's restorative justice [righteousness] is revealed. *And as we will see,* it begins with and ends in faith. As the Scripture declares: "By faith the just will obtain life."[10] (vv. 16–17)

What does it mean to be saved? Rescued? Can you imagine the earth shaking violently beneath your bed? I can hardly imagine the sound; the creaking, the crashing, the swaying of your house. After it stops, you hear screams, some loud and clear, and some muffled. There's nothing clear to you, just darkness and lots of dust. Dust in your eyes, dust in your lungs; maybe you are lucky enough to crawl out of what was once your house; maybe you aren't. Watching the footage of the 2010 Haitian earthquake and looking into the eyes of people who have been literally pulled out of that rubble, you see gratefulness unlike any other, and an enthusiasm for life. Could you imagine being rescued like this and saying to a rescuer, "Where have you *been*? Why didn't you get here sooner? I've been waiting for days!" It would be ridiculous to be ungrateful to the ones who have pulled you out and rescued you from a slow and certain death. Yet many Christians live with this kind of attitude.

You were rescued! You've destroyed your life with sin and you're living in destruction by your own choice. You deserve to die. But God, the Creator, has reached into that destruction with love, saying, "I'm here to pull you out." I hope that you and I would respond like many of the people rescued in the first days after the tragic Haitian quake. Those people, just rescued, some with broken bones, went back to pull other people out. That is who I am called to be. That's who I want to be.

Paul goes on:

For the wrath of God is breaking through from heaven, opposing all *manifestations of* ungodliness and wickedness by the people who do wrong to keep God's truth in check—*they cloak their sin in lies and deceit.* These people are not ignorant about what can be known of God, because He has shown it to them *with great clarity.* From the beginning, creation in its magnificence enlightens us to His invisible nature. Creation itself makes His undying power and divine identity clear, even though they are invisible, and voids their excuses *and ignorant claims* of these people because, despite the fact that they knew the one true God, they have failed to show the *love*, honor, and appreciation due to the One who created them! (vv. 18–21)

We long to gather in a community of people who together say, "May we live in the love, honor, and appreciation of the one who created and rescued us, and being rescued ourselves, may we reach for others both near and far." Friends, we have much to do. I believe we are a people who know, deep within our hearts, that we are made for these moments with our neighbors, with our coworkers, with our friends, with our international brothers and sisters who are suffering. Martin Luther said this about the first chapter of Romans: "There you have it. The gospel is a story about Christ, God's, and David's son who died and was raised and is established as Lord. This is the gospel in a nutshell."[11]

How would you define the gospel?

PRAYER

True God, we thank you for the chance to meet you through your Spirit and through the loving touch and kind words of brothers and sisters. Thank you that you speak to us anew through the Scriptures, especially through the first chapter of Romans. Through these words you allow each one of us to fall in love with you again, because these words point to your love and grace, to the fact that you're a rescuing God. Lord, we long to be the kind of people who, when pulled out of the rubble, come out grateful and thankful, ready to be a part of your rescue mission in this world. We thank you that though we remain in the rubble and in despair because of our own failures, you choose not to hold it against us; instead, you offer your grace and unconditional forgiveness. Thank you for the sacrifice of your son, Jesus the Liberating King. May we be continually reminded of his love as we meet and share with one another. We pray this as one people in your name, in the name of the Father, and of the Son, and of the Holy Spirit. Amen.

Interview with Rick McKinley and Gabe Lyons

Rick and Gabe are two of my dear friends, which is fitting for this discussion that focuses on relationality. When we fail to think about Christianity in relational terms, we easily drift off into religious rituals that are stale and exhausting. It is purposeful that God describes our relationship with covenant marital terminology.

CHRIS: Rick, in your book, *This Beautiful Mess,* you talk about the gospel—that some people believe we are talking about two gospels. On some level there's a sense of God cosmically making things right, restoring all that's broken. And on another level there's this personal declaration that God has made us righteous, that he's imputed the righteousness of Christ. And there's a tendency that we try to allow these two themes to oppose one another rather than to integrate them. Both of us have learned a lot from Lesslie Newbigin on this, and the reality is, these themes of the gospel need to be integrated, and when we identify this kind of dualistic perspective, we can then seek integration. There's a lot of debate going on right now in theological circles about what justification really looks like. What are your thoughts about how we begin to get past that unhealthy thinking?

RICK: There are those dualisms, those polarities, that pull us apart. I look at it and think one of the primary issues is that we're looking through the lens of individuality as opposed to relationality. So, as an individual, I either have imputed righteousness or there's no kind of true individualism, which is the restoration of all creation of which I am a part. It appears to me from reading the New Testament (and the book of John in particular) that we've been caught up into the righteous relationship of the Trinity. So the righteousness that is given to me is ontological; it is deep within my being, but it's only connected to my union with Christ. If I separate myself from that union, then I'm still just Adam [human]. But in this relationship and union where Christ is in me, I am in the Father, you are in me, and the Holy Spirit is with you and will be in you [see John 14, 17]. All of a sudden, there is this love relationship between Father, Son, and Spirit, and we're caught up into that. That's where I would say the gospel is bigger than even the restoration of creation, because if that was the endgame, then we could have another fall in heaven. We're just going to be like Adam again, right?

Or has God done something through the fall that's bigger, (in gaining a bride for the Son), and actually brought us into the union with God the Father, God the Son, God the Spirit, so that we're participating in the divine nature, drinking of Christ in us? He's the head and we're the body; there's this union. At that point we don't sin because we're in Christ and Christ isn't going to sin in the glorified kingdom. I think a lot of the tension comes from this non-Trinitarian, nonrelational understanding of the gospel, where God is just a modality, or just this kind of One Being, the absolute unmoved mover kind of thing. So we're looking for our individual righteousness and we're now just a nonrelational being that needs imputed righteousness in order to be justified before God. Those are perhaps by-products, but they're only understood and experienced and perhaps true through the union with Christ. The minute the relationship disappears, you're left thinking, *I've got to go down this road of religious duties,* because there's no relationship. As opposed to thinking, *Christ has saved me by grace through faith, not of myself, but has prepared works for me to do, so that it's Christ in me doing the work in the world.*

CHRIS: And religious duty is not what Christianity is about.

RICK: No, that's overflow. That's the body metaphor, the wedding metaphor, the marriage metaphor. Paul says in Ephesians 5, "I know this is a mystery, but I'm actually not talking about marriage. I'm talking about Christ and the church. He left the Father to cleave to us" [vs. 32–33]. So I think the question becomes, Are we going to continue to read all relational teaching in Scripture metaphorically? Are we willing to embrace it in actuality?

CHRIS: How can we think of righteousness in a more integrated and relational manner?

GABE: Well, I think people—and it's especially true and ironic for the non-Christian population—have a deep desire to be a part of anything that's restoring this world. There is this innate desire and a longing for grace in each of our lives, for the meaning and purpose that every single human being is trying to find a way to quench. A lot of different religions teach people that they probably cannot quench it, but they can try to mitigate that feeling by trying to achieve some sort of works-based religion or works-based achievement and quench that desire they have. But I think for the Christian, and for those who are spiritually open, curious, and looking for answers, he or she is discovering that through Christ alone can you quench all of that, because it's not something you achieve in terms of accomplishment, but something you achieve in terms of accepting it. In that way, it's not some linear track you're on, trying to reach some intended goal; instead, it's really a state of being and a state of awareness to what Christ is trying to do through us at every given moment, no matter how big or small that might seem to measure by the world's standards.

CHRIS: We've clearly seen our peers push back on the idea of legalistic Christianity, sometimes to the point that they live in a state of overreaction. How do you assess that transformation over the last couple of decades?

GABE: Well, for me, growing up in a more conservative environment, where there were a lot of well-intentioned rules (to keep us out of harm's way and on a good path) that came along with being a Christian, really caused me to underestimate God's grace and the freedom that he wants to give us to experience all the good things of this world that we should enjoy. It put the power back on the human side of control and discipline. Trying to discipline ourselves in a certain way versus understanding that motivation is how most of us live. But when we're motivated by the love of Christ, by the grace of Christ, it actually causes us to live in such a way that we actually become unconcerned about the haircuts, tattoos, and so many other little things that become markers for people as to how spiritual you are. Which, looking back, seems completely ridiculous.

But I've also seen in our generation, among our peers, the pendulum swinging the whole other way, to no discretion, and the assumption that we can do anything, through the freedom of Christ. That we should be able to just do anything and not be thoughtful about it. But I think a healthy balance to that is on an individual basis of what God is calling each of us to do. As human beings, we tend to judge because that's how we can assess who's in and who's out, who we should be hanging out with and who we shouldn't be. So we minimize God's grace down to the lowest common denominator, and it becomes something entirely different than what Christ intended. This reminds me of the Luke 7:36–44 passage, where Jesus and Simon the Pharisee are interacting in Simon's home, and the prostitute comes in and pours out her perfume on Jesus' feet. Simon can't believe that this is happening, because he has lived by the rules, he's understood the rules, and is clearly about the rules. Jesus basically teaches Simon a big lesson using this lady as an example to say, "You know, she's closer on this path for me than you are because she's not living according to these smug rules. She's actually aware and expressing love out of her heart, and it goes way deeper than what you can measure with your dos and don'ts."

CHRIS: Yeah, and this is what Paul is so clear about in Romans, that focusing on the law and on the rules doesn't actually help us to live by the law and the rules. And part of the journey of a Christian—I know the friends and the folks that we've been journeying with have been learning—is that by focusing more on Jesus and partnering with his redemptive work in the world, we have become redeemed and transformed. But it won't happen from external motivation to live by the rules, but by an internal one to be transformed.

GABE: Yeah, I find that it's really about getting the order correct. C. S. Lewis has this great quote where he talks about never getting the right second things if you don't have the proper first things. If we don't put the gospel first and put forward the power of Christ in our lives to be transforming us constantly, then we tend to focus on the second things, which in proper context are just the result of a heart that's completely devoted to him. The whole of these "second things" that we are trying to control, coerce into, or create boundaries for consume us, when in reality our focus should actually be on the first things—a focus on the gospel and the proper understanding of righteousness. Only then can we clearly see these second things manifest themselves in ways that honor and glorify God.

CHRIS: That's exactly it. When in doubt, C. S. Lewis always seems to set us straight.

FOUR

Imago Dei

We are all alike on the inside.
- Mark Twain

I can't help but wonder why You care about mortals—sons and daughters of men—specks of dust floating about the cosmos.
- Psalms 8:4

Carl Sagan articulates a particularly low view of humanity and our place in the universe. He asks, with more than a little angst, "Who are we? We find that we live on an insignificant planet of a humdrum star lost in a galaxy tucked away in some forgotten corner of a universe in which there are far more galaxies than people."[1]

It is interesting to me that both Sagan and I can look out upon the same vast system of stars and galaxies and yet arrive at exactly opposite understandings of what we see. Have you ever taken the time to peruse the amazing photographs of space compiled by NASA? One of these NASA photographs uniquely captures my imagination. It depicts a small galaxy, once thought to be a satellite that orbited our own Milky Way, known as the Large Megallanic Cloud. It is an intricately beautiful dwarf galaxy that can be observed from earth with the naked eye. Calling it a dwarf galaxy makes it sound small, yet it spans a distance of more than fifteen-thousand light-years. Considering this is a small and nearby galaxy, how capacious are the distant expansive galaxies? It is almost unfathomable; to think of it makes my head hurt. Sagan observes this grand universe and feels small. But as I see the vast and amazing handiwork of our Creator God, my faith soars. I find hope and meaning in this amazing cosmos created by his hand. I have an intimate relationship with the One who spoke all of this into existence. For this reason John begins his gospel with a reminder:

> Before time itself was measured, the Voice was speaking. The Voice was and is God. This *celestial* Voice remained ever present with the Creator; His speech shaped the entire cosmos. *Immersed in the practice of creating*, all things that exist were birthed in Him. His breath filled all things with a living, breathing light—light that thrives in the depths of darkness, *blazing through murky bottoms*. It cannot, and will not, be quenched. (John 1:1–5)

If God can set all of these planets in orbit and place the stars perfectly in the sky, surely my mortgage payment is not an obstacle too great for him. As I soak in the beauty, splendor, and majesty of all creation, I feel a new confidence in my step, a renewed trust that God is making all things right.

There is real significance in asking and exploring these important questions about the nature of humanity. Who are we as humans? How are we connected to God? These inquiries nudge us along on the journey of redemption. But if we miss this next question, although we may understand the majority of the gospel according to Jesus, we will find ourselves wandering far from the narrow path. When we understand the nature of humanity, who we are created to be, we are then truly prepared to live an intimately intertwined life with the Creator and accomplish the work he has for us.

Who Are We?

Who are we? Who are we made to be? What does it mean to be human?

I have entered into many awkward moments over the course of my life, but none more uncomfortable than a recent trip to a yoga class at my local gym. It was doubly awkward for me because I am one of the least flexible people on this planet (I have a dream of being able to stand up straight and touch my toes), which is why I was going to this class, because I realize that as you get older, flexibility is equally (if not more) important than building strength. I walked into this yoga class and saw people with their legs wrapped behind their heads. I felt an instant aversion to these remarkably malleable classmates. It was one of those times I wished my cell phone would ring so I could pretend that it was an emergency and just run away. Even more awkward was that I had a very intense yoga instructor who asked me to gaze deeply into her eyes as I entered the class. She put her hands together, bowed, and said, "Namaste." Basically defined, *namaste* means "the divine within me greets and meets the divine within you." The pastor and theologian part of me awakened despite the gentle melodies of Enya, and I had a deep need to clarify.

I pointedly asked if we could pause a moment to define this a bit before the class started. (I bowed as I mumbled my question.) I wanted to clarify where that divine spark comes from, that it's not a part of me, but a reflection of the Creator himself that has come to dwell within me. Until we made that point of clarification, I was very unsettled. This might seem like a subtle distinction, but it is a truly significant distinction that I believe is essential to a healthy understanding of humanity. I just wanted to stretch, breathe, and relax, but I didn't want the teacher and classmates to think that I believe in any way that we are gods ourselves. So now, not only am I that inflexible guy, but also the one trying to engage in a theological discussion during the yoga class. In short, no one liked me.

I have friends who believe that humans are deities, kind of mini-gods. Looking at my own life—even on my best day—it would be hard to construe that I am a god in any way. Sometimes even the same people, when discussing human behavior versus godlike behavior, explain away human failings as animal nature. So to someone who commits a string of infidelities, they might say, "Well, you're just a man, and man is an animal. You do what your instincts tell you to do, and that's okay. You're just an animal." God or animal? Which is it? Because it doesn't seem that we can be both, right?

There's another story being told in our culture. I hear this story everywhere; this story dominates much of the world that we live in. It advances that to be human is to consume. You were made to be here. You were created basically for department stores and shopping centers. Consume all you can; here are some plastic garbage bags so you can conveniently trash what is no longer pleasurable into a giant hole in our planet. This is the lifestyle that believes you can buy your way to happiness, that when you consume you'll reach some kind of Maslowian self-actualization and finally be content with life. Unfortunately, the contentment is designed to be fleeting. "If I can just buy enough . . . If I could just have enough, then I might believe that I have lived enough . . . that I am enough." This is a cycle of consumption that has no end until we discover that nothing outside of God will ever be enough.

One of the reasons that we so quickly fall off course is that we begin to conform to and become a character in one or more of these stories, completely missing the biblical narrative that tells us very clearly who we are and who God created us to be.

We Are Beautiful, Complex, Collaborating Creations

That's who we are. Each of us is created with divinely ordained gifts for God's kingdom. Scripture is infused with the power to lead us into a clearer understanding of human nature. The book of Genesis tells us that we are created "imago dei," in the very image of God (Gen. 1:26). Genesis, rich with the imagery of creation, is a book I love because in it I can clearly hear and feel the nature and voice of our majestic Triune God:

> Eternal God: Now let us conceive *a new creation that sounds the heartbeat of its Creator*, a human, made in our image, fashioned according to our likeness. *So God did just that.* He created humanity in His image, created them male and female, *reflecting God's own relational richness.* Then God blessed them and gave them this directive: *Join me in the ongoing work of creation.* Be fruitful, multiply, and fill the earth *for it needs your tender care and cultivation.* I make you trustees *of my estate*, so rule over the fish of the sea, the birds of the air, and every creature that roams across the face of the earth. (Gen. 1:26–28)

Genesis details much of God's creative process, including the formation of humanity. Often it is said that man is created in God's image in order to be a cocreator. To me this sounds like it oversteps the bounds a little bit. Because of the way that we hear it and understand it, a cocreator seems to suggest a near equality with God, simply a lesser partner in creation. In reality, it is God who first created *all* things, and then commissioned us to obediently participate in his creative work in this world. Genesis certainly calls humans to be collaborators with God in his redemptive work that is reshaping the cosmos according to his will. He has created all that exists, and now he invites us to work with our own entrusted creative gifts to bring about his glory as this narrative continues to unfold, one creative, permitted breath at a time.

What does it look like to collaborate with God, as stated in Genesis 1:26? It means letting God wrap his heart around your own while letting go of the control of your own heart and binding to his passion. It is allowing yourself to be his pulse on the earth, to be filled with his desire to make things new. It is seeing and presenting his view of the world by reflecting his light into every place. Yes, *every place*, no matter how dark. God has given each person specific talents and the ability to utilize them to forward the agenda of his kingdom. We are to follow God as his vision becomes manifest through our humility by putting aside our own personal agendas because God has inspired us to pick up what is broken and form it into something new. We are the active agents of the primary reformation. Ultimately, this fulfills all our dreams and allows us to do what we were truly made to do: not to gluttonously consume, but to gladly collaborate with God in his creative work in this world.

We Are Handmade

So now you see how the Creator swept into being the spangled heavens and earth *in six days*. The canvas *of the cosmos* was completed by day seven, when the True God paused the labor of creating and rested. Thus the Creator blessed day seven *as an open space* designed *for rest and relaxation,* a sacred zone *of Sabbath-keeping,* because God rested from His work that day. (Gen. 2:1–3)

Rest also is a part of your created order. The Sabbath is not just a contemplative ritual; it's a vital part of how you are made. Stillness is a presence-practice, something that helps you meditate on and with God. It becomes a meeting place for God and self. When we slow down to God's restful pace, we are refreshed in ways we cannot measure.

This is the *detailed* story of the Eternal God's *singular work in* creating all that exists. On the day the heavens and earth were created, there were no plants or vegetation to cover the earth. The fields were barren and empty with no life or growth because the Eternal God had not sent the rains *to nourish* the soil or a man to tend the soil. In those days a fog rose from the soil and its vapors irrigated the land. One day He scooped dirt out of the ground, sculpted it into the shape *we call* human, and breathed into the nostrils *of the body to fill the human creation* with life. *When the human body met the divine breath,* a soul was born. (vv. 4–7)

Earthenware. That's us in a nutshell. We were handmade from earth, compressed by God's hands into ecosystems and galaxies of cells and energy within skin. It's incredible to ponder every fine detail of our living bodies, all of which would collapse into a pile of dust had his breath not energized it to life.

The Eternal God planted a garden in the east *and called* it Eden— *for it was a place of utter delight*—and placed the man there. *In this garden* He made the ground pregnant with life—*bursting forth with nourishing food and luxuriant beauty.* He created trees that ravished the eyes and yielded unimaginable delicacies. Among them stood the tree of life. And in the center of this garden *of delights* stood the tree of the knowledge of good and evil. (*But more about that later in the story.*) (vv. 8–9)

Eden itself was evidence of God's creative beauty, and the food God designed to spring out of plants for us is further proof of his power. On this side of Eden, most of us know that food isn't all it was intended to be, due to tragedies like factory farming. I have eaten fruit before that has absolutely no flavor—sometimes tasting like cardboard, sometimes not tasting like anything at all. You can taste a drastic difference if you compare a good organic apple to one sprayed with chemicals. When my wife and I get away, one of the ways we meet God is at a great breakfast buffet piled with fruit from one end of the table to the other. Together, we drink bottomless coffee and eat our fill of fresh mangoes, pineapples, strawberries, and papayas. The garden of Eden was infinitely beyond this in luxury, sweetness, and beauty. Trees ravished the eyes and yielded unimaginable delicacies. Among them stood the Tree of Life, and in the center of this garden of delights stood the Tree of the Knowledge of Good and Evil.[2] But before we can talk about that in detail, we need to discuss the second human God created.

God's creative power and artistic brilliance, according to the opinion of men the world over, is blatantly apparent in his creation of women. Eve was the first, and some theorize that she may have been the most beautiful woman ever.

Not long after, God's voice sounded throughout creation.

Eternal God: It is not good for the man to be alone, so I will create a companion for him, a perfectly molded partner.

Out of the *same* ground *that the man came from,* the Eternal God sculpted animals and birds of every kind. Then He brought them to the man and gave him the authority to name each creature as he saw fit, *thereby making room for humans to participate in God's creative act.* So the man chose names for domesticated animals, birds, and wild beasts. But none of these creatures was a right and proper partner for Adam. (vv. 18–20)

This could be the most significant understatement in all of Scripture. Can you imagine Adam sizing up all the animals? Even man's best friend, the dog, is not the same as having another of your kind to relate with. I can only imagine how many he had given names to before he was feeling disappointed—just didn't ever get that butterflies-in-the-stomach excitement with the anteater or aardvark. Knowing this already, God says, "Don't worry. None of these are a proper partner for you, Adam."

So the Eternal God put the man into a deep sleep, removed a rib *from his side,* and closed the flesh around the opening. He sculpted a woman from the man's rib and presented her to the man. (vv. 21–22)

This is especially significant symbolism. The fact that she was born from the side of the man intimates that she is his equal, a cojoined partner. So we arrive at the big introductory moment for both Adam and Eve. God's been sculpting, making final touches on her hair . . . she's finished. Adam's been asleep, and he starts to stir. You can imagine this moment when they see one another for the first time. It's also their wedding day. She didn't have time to make a dress so she's just standing there, fresh out of God's hands—never seen a human, much less had a thought before—naked before her new husband.

Now, as men, this would be the place you could really, really significantly ruin it. I mean, most of us spend every Valentine's Day apologizing. We miss it. Adam is waking up to the most amazing of gifts, so you can imagine he'd like the first words he speaks to his new, naked bride to be significant. And so he sings. In fact, some believe that it was only after sin entered the world that we began to have words spoken instead of sung, that up until the fall, all of the action in creation was psalm. I resonate with this theory. Adam sings to his wife, and his new bride hears lyrics that rhyme in Hebrew. This is just a glimpse of what he was saying:

Man: *You and I are forever joined together.* We are one flesh, and we share the same bones. I will call you Woman, *as an eternal reminder* that you were taken forth from Man. (v. 23)

It's pretty good. Better than any Hallmark card I've read recently. "You and I are one. We belong together. We cannot be separated."

This is the reason a man leaves his father and his mother, and is united with his wife; and the two *who once lived as "me's"* come together as *"we,"* one flesh *and blood. In those days* the man and his wife were both naked and were not ashamed. (vv. 24–25)

Genesis also describes the four rivers that flowed through the garden, then addresses the very first commandment God gave man:

I will make you and your brood enemies of the woman and all her children; the woman's child will stomp your head, and you will bite his heel.

(*to the woman*): *As a consequence of your actions,* I am increasing your suffering—the pain of labor at childbirth and the sorrow of bringing forth the next generation. You will desire a husband; *but rather than a companion and collaborator,* he will be the dominant partner.

(*to the man*): Because you followed your wife's advice *instead of My command* to refrain from the fruit I had forbidden you to eat, cursed is the ground. For the rest of your life, you will fight for every crumb of food from the *crusty clump of* clay *I made you from.* (Gen. 3:15–17)

God created humans for this beauty, this place of rest, where husband and wife exist together in tropical bliss. They lie around naked and eat fruit. *This* is what they do. *This* is what they were made for. But as we know, sin entered the world. Eve, the daughter of creation, goes from bliss (a buffet of fruit and one simple rule: just don't eat from the one tree) to a fallen world, where she becomes a mother who will not only experience pain during childbirth, but who will be deeply devastated by the pain sin will cause through her sons.

We were made in God's image, reflecting his energy, his beauty, his character. We were made for the Garden and bliss and perfection and unity with God. But because of sin, we are no longer denizens of a perfect world, but one that is lush with brokenness. We are no longer naked, clothed by God alone, but are hidden under clothes, toughened by the world around us. It's no good. It's bitter. And in the midst of murder, despair, and separation from God, our identity and what we were made for becomes foggy and indistinct.

We Are Collected in Him

Jesus steps in, and in his presence says, "I am here to restore what has been broken—the *imago dei* that is shattered. I'll enter and I'll begin to put the pieces together." Through his saving act, he is gathering us up into himself, collecting the fragments and creating a bride of his own. Although still broken, because of him we begin to reflect the beauty of God once again. The divine spark does not come from within us; we reflect into the world the character and the nature of God as it shines upon us, through us, and off us. It's quite an important difference. In Romans 8 Paul says,

> Therefore, now no condemnation awaits those who are living in Jesus, the Liberating King, [avoiding sin and embracing the Spirit,] because when you live in Him *a new law takes effect*. The law of the Spirit of life breathes into you and rescues you from the law of sin and death. God did something the law could never do. *You see, human flesh took its toll on God's law. In and of itself the law is not weak,* but the flesh weakens it. So to condemn the sin that was ruling in the flesh, God sent His own Son, bearing the likeness of sinful flesh, as a sin offering. (vv. 1–3)[3]

It would be easy to fall into thinking that the flesh is bad and the spiritual is good, but this is not true. God is actually illuminating and redeeming the flesh itself. God created it all and he is redeeming it all.

> Now we are able to live up to the justice demanded by the law. But that ability has not come from living by our fallen human nature; it has come because we walk according to the movement of the Spirit in our lives.
>
> If you live your life animated by the flesh—*namely, your fallen, corrupt nature*—then your mind is focused on the matters of the flesh. But if you live your life animated by the Spirit—*namely, God's indwelling presence*—then your focus is on the work of the Spirit. A mind focused on the flesh is doomed to death, but a mind focused on the Spirit will find full life and complete peace. (vv. 4–6)

If we focus on laws, or following all the rules, or chasing worldly indulgences, or worrying about things we cannot control, we will continually fail. But if we focus on the Spirit, asking God to dwell within us, to speak through us, then God begins to illuminate us and transforms our focus to the work of the Spirit. A mind focused on the flesh (rules) is doomed to death, but a mind focused on the Spirit (personality of God) will find fullness in life and complete peace. These are comforting words:

> You see, a mind focused on the flesh is declaring war against God; it defies the authority of God's law and is incapable of following His path. *So it is clear that* God takes no pleasure in those who live oriented to the flesh.
>
> But you do not live in the flesh. You live in the Spirit, assuming of course that the Spirit of God lives inside of you. *The truth is that* anyone who does not have the Spirit of the Liberator living within does not belong to God. If the Liberating King lives in you, then *God's restorative* justice is breathing life into your spirits despite the fact that sin brings death to your bodies. If the Spirit of the One who resurrected Jesus from the dead lives inside of you, then *you can be sure that* He will cast *the light of* life into your mortal bodies through the life-giving power of the Spirit residing in you.
>
> So, my brothers and sisters, you owe the flesh nothing! (Romans 8: 7–12)

The unfortunate truth is that most of us are living as slaves. We're slaves to money, sex, power, or romantic love. And people who have carefully avoided those snares are often stuck trying to follow all the religious rules, which, as we see above, doesn't lead to a free life either. But we *can* be truly free. In describing God's flashy slave deliverance in the Bible, Walter Brueggemann, an Old Testament theologian, says that the Jews' exodus from slavery in Egypt began with understanding that they owed Pharaoh nothing.[4]

The good news is that Creator God is still in the business of the prison break. We, too, must understand that whatever is ruling us—money, sex, power, rules, this emperor, this pharaoh, this earthly king—we are not indebted to in any way. We can be truly free because that's the price that's been paid. We owe the flesh nothing, Paul says. The indwelling personality of God can finally free us of any addiction or master: "You do not need to live according to its ways, *so abandon its oppressive regime.* For if your life is just about satisfying the impulses of your sinful nature, then prepare to die" (Rom. 8:12–13).

Could it be clearer? Paul says the life that so many of us are leading is just about getting what we want today. We get up and pursue it, but it simply leads to death.

But if you have invited the Spirit to destroy these selfish desires, you will experience life. If the Spirit of God is leading you, then *take comfort in knowing you are His children.* You see, you have not received a spirit that returns you to slavery, so you have nothing to fear. The spirit you have welcomes you into God's own family. You have been adopted, *and God is truly your Father.* That's why we call out to Him, "Abba! Father!" *as we would address a loving daddy.* (Romans 8: 13–15)

Often we begin to wonder, *What does it look like to be fully human?* What would Adam have been like, and Eve, if the Garden had not been lost? What would be going on? What would they be doing? How would they engage? What would life and marriage and culture look like if humanity had not fallen? We have only one place to find out: in the life and the actions of Jesus. As we reflect, we need to ask God to change our character to be likened to Jesus, the only human that is fully restored, fully human, yet fully God.

> *From the distant past,* His eternal love reached into the future, and He chose those who would be conformed to the image of His Son. *God not only knew which part they would play, but He chose them* especially to be united with His Son, the firstborn of a new family of believers, all brothers and sisters. All His chosen ones have been called to a different destiny to experience what it means to be justified and glorified together. (Rom. 8:29–30)

As we think of what's going on in the world, if we take the *imago dei* seriously—that all are created in the image of God— we are all challenged to live in a radically new way. Most of the great evils that exist in the world undermine the *imago dei.* Any way that we distort humanity by elevating or lowering one person over another is sin. The ways that we treat the elderly or the unborn, the disabled or poor . . . you don't have to go very far to find examples of it. When people continue to try and craft their way into perfection, we reject what we view as ugly and strive to be an "elevated being" or to be physically perfect. We push and pull ourselves up or down at any given moment, trying to find our place, where we fit. We cannot be pupils of Jesus unless we are willing to drop our own desperate attempts to fix ourselves, turn in acceptance and humility, and begin to truly learn, to take instruction. To love God, you will care for all people. What about the physically, mentally and emotionally broken? Yes. All people. Because if we believe what the Scriptures say, we cannot deny they are also image bearers of the Creator. We must treat humanity in a different way. We must stand up for life in every way. In this way, our character is being conformed to Jesus.

Take time to reflect and to examine your sin. Ask God to change and transform you. Take some things off; put other things on.

Saint Augustine's *Confessions* radically changed the way people see the world. It was and is historic for the way it shifted perspective and developed our Western worldview. In one of the first chapters of the book, he summarizes the journey that allows us to see the fullness of humanity and to understand what it means to be holistically spiritual. One of my all-time favorite quotes is from Saint Augustine: "You've made us for Yourself, Lord. And our hearts are restless until they rest in You." That is what we want to express— that we are made for God and we will be restless (and we will mess up, and we will fail miserably) until we strip back our own-ness, our comforts, our distractions, our diversions . . . until we learn to rest in God.

PRAYER

Lord, we thank you that you created all things. You created man and woman as equals, equally created in your image, reflecting your glory and your beauty. In our fallenness, too often we fail to reflect your character. God, help us to see who we were created to be and to see that the work you do within us redeems and changes us. Transform us to be more and more like you. To love the way that you love. To be generous with our things the way you were generous with your things. To see the true beauty, hope, and potential in hurting and outcast people. To love the children and the weak and the helpless in the way you love them. To see the sick and believe that you have called us to be a part of their healing journey. We pray for our culture that is filled with disparity, hate, and anger about what it means to care for the sick. We pray that the church would simply *be* the church. We long for all who are sick and those who are in need of medical care to be healed through your power, through your grace, and through the blessings that you have given us.

Give us eyes to see what you see and faith that illuminates us and leads us to follow. It is your Spirit that dwells within us. We are not in and of ourselves divine, but we reflect your divine nature and pray that it would be evident to those around us, to this locality and to the world. We celebrate a new righteousness that's found in you. It can't be found in our attempt to live by the rules; it can't be found in our pursuit of morality, and it would never be found in a religious spirit that looks down on others. It is found only in your love and grace and forgiveness and through the transforming power of your

Spirit that enters our hearts. We pray this together, united as one family, adopted into your family by our loving and perfect Parent. We share one baptism and one faith. We pray in the name of the Father, the Son, and the Holy Spirit. Amen.

Interview with Shane Claiborne

Shane Claiborne has devoted his life to seeing the image of God at work in places that we easily ignore it. The way he sees God in the face of Iraqi children or troubled teens in South Philly is a perfect example of the *imago dei* in action.

CHRIS: Shane, if our pursuit of justice is rooted in the *imago dei*, and if we believe God is seeking justice as a means to restore all things, then it is natural that we are made to desire a world that is made right. Are you concerned that many separate justice from Christian faith?

SHANE: Yeah, one of the really powerful images for this idea of justice I got when I was in Iraq. I met this guy who said his name was Adal, which in Arabic means "justice." He was explaining his idea of justice to me, and he said it's like the scales are balanced. He said *balance* or *justice* or *shalom* are all the same thing. He was explaining this to me, and in that very moment, this little Iraqi kid runs up and hands me a flower. Adal said, "Like flowers . . . if we give flowers, like the children, then we will receive flowers in the life to come." Then he pointed to the air where the smoke was coming from the bombs that were falling, "And if we bring bombs on earth, then we get fire in the world to come."

I thought, *Man, that sounds a lot like Jesus,* this idea that if you pick up the sword, you die by the sword. So much of our Scripture is warning us of the consequences of shalom. If we do something out of balance, if we do something that's unjust, it will eventually bite us back. There's a beautiful place in Scripture where Jesus says, "judge not lest ye be judged" [Matt. 7:1], and I think that's the real idea we get out of this. I don't know how we miss mercy triumphing over judgment and that we're not to judge others. We make it very literal and so esoteric that it becomes, "Don't judge people or else God's going to judge you when you die." When we walk around pointing fingers at other people, more fingers are pointing back to us. Part of the problem has to do with evangelical leaders that have spoken out about gay people, sexual morality, and the like; then they do something wrong and the fire comes. So, judge not, lest you be judged, and as much as you judge, you, too, will be judged. And as much as you forgive, you shall be forgiven.

In another beautiful story, Jesus interrupts the scene where the woman was caught in adultery and is getting ready to be stoned. It is a capital crime that gives every legal right to kill her, yet Jesus interrupts and basically says, "You're all adulterers, you're all murderers, if you've looked at someone lustfully, if you've called someone a fool. Let the person without sins be the first to cast a stone." The stones start to fall to the ground, and the only person left with the right to throw a stone (Jesus) has no inclination to do so. If that doesn't teach us that the closer we are to God, the less we are to throw stones at other people, then I don't know what does.

I think that restorative justice is a fantastic translation of *diakasanu,* "righteousness," because that's what we're led to do: to repair what's been broken and to interrupt the patterns of injustice. So the work that's bringing victims and offenders together in prisons is restorative justice. That is some of the most redemptive work, because people see the humanity in the brokenness of each other. And they hear, although not necessarily from the exact person they committed a crime against, what it feels like to be robbed at gunpoint or sexually assaulted, and something happens when you break through that. That's what penitentiaries were supposed to be about. Some of the first ones in Pennsylvania were started with the idea of repentance. Penance involves thinking about what we've done and how we were living so that we can be restored into society, not so we are warehoused forever.

I remember a letter I got from a guy in prison who wrote (he had read some of my books), telling me that he was alive today because of grace. He had done something bad, but the family of the victim said he was better than that awful thing he had done, that he shouldn't be killed for what he had done. They even argued on his behalf against the death penalty. Being in prison gave him a lot of time (literally) to think about grace, to think about God's love and justice; and eventually he became a Christian in prison. That should call all of us Christians who are leading the war drums around the death penalty to really challenge ourselves to think about how Jesus feels about the death penalty. Jesus was asked, and his answer was, "Let the person without sin cast the first stone."

God's restorative justice is bigger than our mistakes. God is able to make up for the stupid things we do, and it doesn't mean that they're taken lightly. It doesn't mean that we don't take evil seriously or don't think that sin destroys and hurts people. David is a good example—a man after God's own heart who broke pretty much every commandment, yet Solomon was born and the lineage of Jesus continued. God always makes something out of the messes we make.

CHRIS: That is so true. God created a world of beauty, and we messed it up. But he did not pull out and abandon us. In fact, he did just the opposite. He entered into the messed-up world to restore it, to bring forgiveness and shalom.

FIVE

We Fell,
but Can We Get Up?

Man is the only animal that blushes. Or needs to.
— Mark Twain

God's image is present in every human being. There are no exceptions to this truth. Contemplate that for a minute: Adolf Hitler was an image bearer of God. Charles Manson was made in God's own image. Jeffrey Dahmer carried the image of God within him at all times. Pol Pot, same. You and I, at both our best and our worst, are made to reflect the love, grace, and beauty of the God who created all that exists, and who made it all out of thin air. So if we are made to be mirrors that reflect the nature of God, how can we also be so sinful and depraved? These two do not seem to go together well. How is it that we are capable of tremendous evil if we were shaped to contain a spark of the divine? Can that spark become lost or permanently hidden from the world?

The story of Genesis explains it all, but we have often reduced the Genesis narrative to a CliffsNotes version of theology. We focus on our conclusions (we like to call them facts) rather than the story. We acknowledge the impact of the fall, that sin entered the world, but we don't really understand what *sin* means. The definition of *sin* handed to me from the church was that God has established his law, and I miss the mark as I fail to live up to his commands. In my mind, I reduced this teaching to: sin = doing bad things. As my understanding of sin progressed, I expanded that definition to include sins of omission: sin = the things that I fail to do. But it all revolved around rule keeping. N. T. Wright correctly connects our "missing of the mark" to the *imago dei*, and how at that point, our perception of human sin begins to come into focus. He says:

> It is clear that all humans (other than Jesus) do in fact perform acts which constitute a refusal of the vocation to be genuinely, God-reflectingly human, and which therefore "miss the mark" of that lovely, fully human life which is not only glorifying to God in itself but which reflects that glory powerfully and creatively into the world.[1]

Sin is about relationships, not about rules. We are meant to reflect God, and if we are to do that, there must be an unobstructed connection in our relationship to God. Think of it this way: We function much like the satellite dish that is mounted to my roof. If the dish is pointed in the wrong direction or blocked by branches or clouds, it will not reflect the image it was intended to receive. All I will see is static. Humanity is similar; sin skews the angle and blocks the reception of the image we were made to receive and reflect. We see in Genesis that when humanity chooses to embrace sin, there are cosmic and eternal consequences. But we distance ourselves from the relational dynamic of the story of Genesis by lifting the facts up and out of the narrative, focusing on propositions, and in doing so we distort the truth and miss the monumental impact of the relational fracture between God and man. If we fail to see sin as a splinter that severs a relationship that was robust, healthy, and whole, then we are able to minimize sin. Sin is relational. In order to sin against God, we must first be in relationship with him. The original story in paradise began to unfold, or unravel, like this:

Of all the wild creatures the Eternal God had created, the serpent was the craftiest.

Serpent: *Dear woman*, is it true that God has forbidden you to eat fruits from the trees of the garden?

Woman: *No, serpent. He said* we may eat *freely. We are granted access to any variety and all amounts* of fruit in the garden with one exception—the fruit from the tree found in the center of the garden. God instructed us not to eat or touch the fruit of this tree, so we would not experience certain death.

Serpent: *Die?* No, you would not die. *God is playing games with you. The truth is,* God knows eating the fruit from that tree will awaken something powerful in you and make you like Him: possessing *all* knowledge of things both good and evil.

The woman *approached the tree,* eyed its fruit, and coveted its *mouth-watering, wisdom-granting* beauty. She plucked a fruit from the tree and ate. She then offered the fruit to her husband, and he ate as well. Suddenly their eyes were opened *to a reality previously unknown.* For the first time, they *sensed their vulnerability and rushed* to hide their naked bodies, stitching fig leaves into a crude loincloth. Just then, they heard the Eternal God walking in the cool shadows of the garden. They took cover among the trees.

Eternal God (*calling to the man*): Where are you?

Man: I was hiding from You. I was afraid when I heard You coming.

Eternal God: *Why are you afraid?*

Man: Because I am naked.

Eternal God: Who told you that you are naked? Have you eaten from the tree *in the center of the garden,* the one I commanded you not to eat from?

Man *(pointing at the woman): It was she!* The woman You gave to me put the fruit in my hands, and I ate it.

Eternal God *(to the woman):* What have you done?

Woman: It was the serpent! He tricked me, and I ate. (Gen. 3:1–13)

Shame. Guilt. Embarrassment. Blame. Temptation often snares our pride with promises to know the great mysteries and possess knowledge that will make us like God, or give us power. So sin—as you see it in your own story and in Genesis—is rooted in selfishness; it is an expression of narcissism. In letters and sermons, Augustine explained the problem of sin as *homo incurvatis in se* ("humanity curved in on itself"), and Luther concurred that sin bent the mirror within us that was intended to reflect the image of God. When thinking of humanity as a mirror intended to reflect the *imago dei,* we often mistakenly believe that the fall of man shattered that mirror. Do you know the frustration of dealing with broken glass—hundreds of small shards and fragments, agonizing to clean up, much less attempt to put back together? If the mirror had been shattered, it would seem impossible to restore. But the mirror was not shattered by the fall; it was bent and curved at odd angles that reflect back rather than up. Now, if you can picture it, the curved mirror reflects upon itself. Have you ever stood between two mirrors? Were you puzzled by the wormhole it creates? It mirrors an image, but it sends back a distorted view.

We are beings created for relationships, seeking and longing for restored relations with God and one another. But our curve has disabled our relational capacity; we focus on ourselves when we should be seeking the good in others. Because of our innate relational nature, Matt Jenson says sin should be understood "as a violation, perversion and refusal of those relationships,"[2] and thus we struggle for a purpose, trying anything and everything to "feel right." Sinning is not about doing bad things or forgetting to do good things; being sinful means that we are warped in a way that fractures all of our relationships.

As a pastor, I have a front-row seat for the greatest joys and the most painful tragedies that life may bring our way. I see the way that our warped human nature hurts our families, friends, churches, and even the environment. For me, there is nothing that fans the flame of love more than standing in an intimate triangle as a bride and groom pledge their love to one another. At weddings I get to watch a miracle firsthand as two individuals become one flesh. But the pendulum often swings the other direction when I see the same people indiscriminately hurt the ones they love most.

My home church, Ecclesia, is a community that knows about the loss of sons; we have endured the great pain of burying our own children. On one such occasion I stood with a beloved sister, a faithful single mother whose teenage son was murdered and taken cruelly from this world. I'll never forget the graveside service, where she pushed her way toward the casket as it sank into the ground. She was bellowing out in these deep-seated screams from the very core of her being. I have never heard anything like it. It rattled bones. In her grief and anguish, she seemed determined to reach into the ground as if she was either going to pull him out or join him. Her pain is something I will never forget; everyone left there shaken. Those screams changed me. I will never hug my children the same way. This is a pain that Eve knew as sin began to transform the world she lived in. A blast of pain suddenly entered her family when one of her sons murdered the other. What a world, right? Only years before, she was lingering, picking fruit, lounging naked with her husband, and strolling with God. Suddenly, tragically, she is experiencing the most devastating kind of grief a mother could know. Imagine the mortal blow of finding out that your son is a murderer, that he took the life of another human being. But what if your son had not murdered a stranger, but instead took the life of your only other son? In reality Eve lost two sons on that day, and she must have wondered why she chose to eat of that fruit. Leading the way for mothers to come, she was tortured with guilt and blame for things that she could not prevent and did not directly cause. Genesis tells the story this way:

Now Adam and Eve discovered the pleasures of lovemaking, and soon Eve conceived and gave birth *to a son whom they named* Cain.

Eve *(excited)*: Look, I have created a new human with the help of the Eternal.

Eve then went on to give birth to Cain's brother, Abel. Abel grew up to become a shepherd, and Cain grew up to become a farmer. After he had learned *how to produce food from the fields,* Cain gave the Eternal One an offering—some of the *grains and* fruits *he had grown* from the ground. For his part Abel gave God some tender *lamb* meat—the choicest cuts from the firstborn of his flock. So The Eternal One accepted Abel and his gift *of lamb,* while he had no regard for Cain and what he presented. Because of this, Cain became angry and his face darkened *with rage. The Eternal One noticed and confronted him.*

Eternal God: Why are you so angry? And why do you look so despondent? *Don't you know* that as long as you do what is right *from a good heart* I accept you? But if you do not do what is right, *watch out because* sin is lurking at the door, ready to pounce on you! You must master it, *before it masters you. Already vengeance is eating at your heart, and it will consume you from the inside.*

Cain went to look for his brother.

Cain *(to Abel)*: Let's take a walk in the field.

When they were in the field, Cain's *envy of his brother got the better of him, and he* killed Abel. (Gen. 4:1–8)

Have you felt the sting of death? Sin is grievous, malevolent, evil, despicable, excruciating, painful, ugly, agonizing, ravaging, and worse than words can possibly portray. In fact, think of the worst thing you can imagine and I guarantee you there is still something worse. So if sin brings so much darkness with it, do you think God has to add on additional penalties to deter us from sin? Is hell a threat to keep us out of trouble? Does God seek to punish those who fail and fall into patterns of sin and destruction? Or is it more like farming? It all comes back to this simple lesson learned in the garden: you reap what you sow. A relationship with God and fellow humans can be beautiful and satisfying, but it can also cause great pain. Every tree produces its own proper fruit. The fruit of righteousness is shalom (more to come in chapter 8 on this important concept from the Hebrew Scriptures), the fruit of the avocado tree is a buttery delicacy called the avocado, and the fruit of sin is death.

There is great debate within parts of the church about the existence of hell and the permanence of suffering. The modern obsession with hell on the part of many evangelicals and the many ways hell is graphically depicted as a means to manipulate or scare people into faith has led many to doubt that such a place exists. To be honest, I do not think the hell depicted to me as a child, a place of eternal burning and constant physical anguish (think: Abu Ghraib for eternity), accurately portrays the biblical understanding of hell. But I do believe in hell, because sin severs our relationship with God. We are not able to spend eternity with God (the source of life) if we are afflicted by sin (the source of death). We have heard hell described with devils, pitchforks, and burning flesh, but we should see that the fullness of our spiritual isolation (being separated from God for eternity) is much more devastating than physical pain. As we ponder the nature of humanity and the effects of sin, we will see the power that sin has to devastate the things we were created to enjoy most.

Keep Your Hands Clean

Our obsession with sin avoidance has not actually helped us to avoid sin. We have chosen to define ourselves by keeping certain rules, but in reality, the more we focus on trying to keep the rules, the more we fixate on breaking them. I would suggest that my denominational tradition, Baptist, would be the foremost among Christian denominations to advocate for marriage and against divorce. I think, more than other denominations, Baptists clearly teach divorce is wrong. We have been known to ostracize and punish those who choose to end their marriage without clear biblical grounds, and we have spent untold fortunes lobbying against gay marriage because it is seen as a threat to biblical unions. So why, then, do Baptists lead the way of all major denominations with 29 percent of marriages ending in divorce, a much higher percentage than the less dogmatic Lutherans and Catholics, who lag behind them with a 21 percent divorce rate?[3] Something is not working.

In his groundbreaking book *Divine Conspiracy*, Dallas Willard says:

> Should we not at least consider the possibility that this poor result is not in spite of what we teach and how we teach, but

precisely because of it? Might that not lead to our discerning why the power of Jesus and his gospel has been cut off from ordinary human existence, leaving it adrift from the flow of his eternal kind of life?"[4]

Interesting thought, right? The problem is not that we need to stand stronger against the social ills and sins; in fact, the way we are standing strong against these evils might be part of the problem. We are against sin, but as we discover in this book, we do not even understand the key tenets of our faith. Ask your friends to define sin for you before you read the rest of this chapter. Is their definition strictly about breaking the cosmic rules? Have they (or you) ever heard of Augustine's and Luther's teaching of *homo incurvatis in se*, that our mirrors are bent inward? Maybe our lack of understanding, not our lack of resolve, is the problem. Willard explains:

> The current situation in which faith professed has little impact on the whole of life, is not unique to our times, nor is it a recent development. But it is currently at an acute stage. History has brought us to the point where the Christian message is thought to be *essentially* concerned *only* with how to deal with sin: with wrongdoing or wrong-being and its effects. Life, our actual existence, is not included in what is now presented as the heart of the Christian message, or it is included only marginally. That is where we find ourselves today.[5]

When our focus on avoiding sin is successful in allowing us to keep our hands clean, we often feel a sense of pride at our accomplishment. Thus sin has entered through the back door, and if you know anything about the sin of religious pride, it is the most toxic poison that one can inject into a relationship. Jesus wisely exploits the dangers of religious pride in the story of the prodigal son. In this story he explains that keeping the rules may be the most sinful state imaginable; it may sever relationships much more severely than breaking the rules. Hear the story as told by Jesus:

Once there was this man who had two sons. One day the younger son came to his father and said, "Father, eventually I'm going to inherit my share of your estate. Rather than waiting until you die, I want you to give me my share now." And so the father *liquidated assets and* divided them. A few days passed and this younger son gathered all his wealth and set off on a journey to a distant land. Once there he wasted everything he owned on wild living. He was broke, a terrible famine struck that land, and he felt desperately hungry and in need. He got a job with one of the locals, who sent him into the fields to feed the pigs. The young man felt so miserably hungry that he wished he could eat the slop the pigs were eating. Nobody gave him anything.

So he had this moment of self-reflection: *"What am I doing here?* Back home, my father's hired servants have plenty of food. Why am I here starving to death? I'll get up and return to my father, and I'll say, "Father, I have done wrong—wrong against God and against you. I have forfeited any right to be treated like your son, but I'm wondering if you'd treat me as one of your hired servants?" So he got up and returned to his father. The father looked off in the distance and saw the young man returning. He felt compassion for his son and ran out to him, enfolded him in an embrace, and kissed him.

The son said, "Father, I have done a terrible wrong in God's sight and in your sight too. I have forfeited any right to be treated as your son."

But the father turned to his servants and said, "Quick! Bring the best robe we have and put it on him. Put a ring on his finger and shoes on his feet. Go get the fattest calf and butcher it. Let's have a feast and celebrate because my son was dead and is alive again. He was lost and has been found." So they had this huge party.

Now the man's older son was still out in the fields working. He came home at the end of the day and heard music and dancing. He called one of the servants and asked what was going on. The servant said, "Your brother has returned, and your father has butchered the fattest calf to celebrate his safe return."

The older brother got really angry and refused to come inside, so his father came out and pleaded with him to join the celebration. But he argued back, "Listen, all these years I've worked hard for you. I've never disobeyed one of your orders. But how many times have you even given me a little goat to roast for a party with my friends? Not once! *This is not fair!* So this son of yours comes, this wasteful delinquent who has spent your hard-earned wealth on loose women, and what do you do? You butcher the fattest calf from our herd!"

The father replied, "My son, you are always with me, and all I have is yours. Isn't it right to join in the celebration and be happy? This is your brother we're talking about. He was dead and is alive again; he was lost and is found again!" (Luke 15:11–32)

Both of these sons are messed up, right? I mean, none of us wants to have a child that blows our family fortune on wine, women, and song. But at least that son came home and the relationship was restored. He caused his father so much pain, but he also brought him great joy. The older son kept the rules, but his sense of entitlement and the anger seeping out of his daily interactions was toxic. Jesus told this story to a group of Pharisees who took great pride in their ability to keep the rules; they were known for making pious statements like, "Heaven rejoices when a sinner is condemned to hell," or "Thank you, God, that I am not like that man." The Son of God had news for them; heaven is not at all rejoicing when a sinner is condemned to hell. Truth be told, God would leave heaven itself (much like a shepherd would leave ninety-nine sheep) to pursue one that is lost. The younger son was lost, but he experienced the beauty described by John Newton, the great hymn writer: "Amazing grace, how sweet the sound, that saved a wretch like me. I once was lost, but now I am found. I was blind, but now I see."

The older brother remains unconvinced that he has ever been or ever will be a wretch, and thus he is intolerable as a son, brother, or human being. None of us like being with people like the older brother. You know the kind of person I am talking about, right? The kind of person who reads the Bible, not to hear God speak to him about love, grace, and sin, but to gain information that will help him in his arguments. No one like likes this person. If you see him walking down the street, you turn and go the other way. His anger and negativity can set your day on the wrong path. I doubt this guy's mom even likes him. The sad truth is, as much as we despise this guy or this girl, we have been there. In fact, even as I write this, and even as you read this, we are likely picturing specific judgmental people we know and are judging them. We look down on them. Welcome to the club. It's amazing how we all drift quite naturally toward the sin of the Pharisees. We enjoy the fleeting rush of looking down our noses at the unenlightened or the unkind. We would be better off in the pig trough—at least then we might realize how lost we truly are.

Jesus is quite clever (an understatement) in telling this story. He is holding up a mirror that allows us to see our folly in both pride and sloth, and they both look pretty ugly. He was just telling a story, but that story pointedly confronts the sin of the Pharisees and our sin. In the Bible, some images of Jesus show a composed man, very stately and kind and gentle. He was tender with the children as they came, and he taught them. But in general, when Jesus faced religious people, he appeared to be a madman. Can you imagine any of us getting so frustrated that we'd go into a place and start turning over tables and throwing a whip around like Indiana Jones? This is what Jesus was up to when he dealt with religious people. "You people are like empty tombs," he'd say. "You've been washed on the outside, but you smell like a rotten body inside." This is not really a friendly warning, not something you can put on a greeting card. He was not much for flowery language.

Jesus was passionate in his pursuit of truth, and he was very clear about it. In Matthew, Jesus warns the disciples to "be careful; avoid the leaven of the Pharisees and Sadducees" (16:6). He is adamant that a little bit of religion, a little bit of condemnation, a looking-down-the-nose at others will spread through the whole loaf just as yeast gives rise to baking bread. The sin Jesus seems to be most aggressively opposing is the sin of pride, specifically religious pride. This is at the heart of the gospel according to Jesus. Friends, may we never be the people believing we are better than others. We are sinners saved by grace; none of us deserve to be rescued. So, if no one is deserving, no one gets to be better-than. This is the problem with religion. It's easy to drift onto that path, so Jesus gives us a clear warning: "Don't go there. You are made to reflect my image, not celebrate how good you are." Peter learned this lesson vividly during an evening boat ride with the disciples:

> Immediately, Jesus made the disciples get into the boat and go on to the other side of the sea while He dismissed the crowd. Then, after the crowd had gone, Jesus went up to a mountaintop alone (*as He*

had intended from the start.) As evening descended, He stood alone on the mountain, praying. The boat was in the water, some distance from land, buffeted and pushed around by waves and wind.

Deep in the night, *when He had concluded His prayers*, Jesus walked out on the water to His disciples *in their boat*. The disciples saw a figure moving toward them and were terrified.

Disciple: It's a ghost!

Another Disciple: A ghost? *What will we do?*

Jesus: Be still. It is I. You have nothing to fear.

Peter: Lord, if it is really You, then command me to meet You on the water.

Jesus: *Indeed*, come.

Peter stepped out of the boat onto the water and began walking toward Jesus. But when he remembered how strong the wind was, his courage caught in his throat and he began to sink.

Peter: Master, save me!

Immediately Jesus reached for Peter and caught him.

Jesus: O you of little faith. Why did you doubt *and dance back and forth between following Me and heeding fear?*

Then Jesus and Peter climbed in the boat together, and the wind became still. And the disciples worshiped Him.

Disciples: Truly You are the Son of God. (Matt. 14:22–33)

Have you been there? Have you experienced a miraculous moment when you were reflecting the beauty of the Creator and being the person you were made to be? It happens sometimes when I am preaching, counseling, writing, or parenting; I experience the joy of God working through me, and it amazes me. Too often I pause, much like Peter, to contemplate the enormity of the situation, the many failures that loom about me, and the disastrous consequences of my potential failure. It only takes that long, a virtual split second, and I have taken my eyes off Jesus and placed them on myself. Like Peter, my mirror is bent inward, but, like Peter, you and I can be fully restored by the grace of God.

PRAYER

God, we see the ways that our internal mirrors have curved in on themselves, and how we are constantly gauging ourselves. We're stuck on ourselves. We seek selfish gain. We use people for our own means rather than nurturing relationships sustained by your love. We have run away from the homeland, from a right dependence on you, and chosen instead to try and make our own salvation. We're helpless, but we are not hopeless. Forgive us again. Please pick us up out of the stormy waters, that we may seek to reflect your love and grace once again. We pray this in the name of the Father, and of the Son, and of the Holy Spirit. Amen.

Interview with Alan Hirsch and Mark Batterson

Alan Hirsch is an Aussie whose writings and ministry have been a gift to the church in Europe and the United States. This conversation with Mark might offer an insight that could keep you from running in circles.

CHRIS: Alan and Mark, my main question for you is about the tendency for many of us to fear that if we take our focus off the righteousness of the Pharisees (keeping the rules and doing all those things), we are going to drift deeper into sin. Paul seems to say he knows it's counterintuitive, but the more we focus on sin, the more trouble we are going to get in, but by focusing on Jesus, we'll be in better shape. We all try to explain what Paul says, but we struggle to grasp it. What can you offer to understand this unique counterintuitive struggle with rules and the gospel?

ALAN: What is interesting is that this idea relates to anxiety: the more you focus on the anxiety you're experiencing, the more anxious you'll become. It's looking not to ourselves but to Jesus to do the righteous work in us, to do his magic in us. I think it is less work, less eyes on ourselves I am very much an activist. I believe we need to be action oriented, to engage in the world—not just praying for it, but actually engaging—and that has got to come out of something rich in our relationship with God. If we shift away from the sense that God does his work in us first, and that remains primary, then I think we end up in the place of Pharisees. I think it's very simple for us to go there. The temptation is very real for spiritual people to get all religious. I think we have to have great sympathy for the Pharisees. I argue that anyone who has been a Christian for five years should read the gospel as if they were the Pharisees. They are more like us than we care to think about. I think we've got to be re-evangelized all the time, don't you, bro? We've got to constantly hear the gospel again and again.

CHRIS: Mark, I love your quote from your book *Primal*. You wrote: "The greatest risk is taking no risk and it's not just risky, it's wrong. And righteousness is using all of our God-given gifts to their full God-given potential. Love doesn't play it safe, it takes risks. Love doesn't make excuses, it takes responsibility. Love doesn't see problems, it seizes opportunities."

MARK: I think for me, and for many, Dallas Willard and his gospel of sin management sparked something in me years ago. It's become a kind of personal mantra for me that is obviously expressed in some of my books and in some of my writings. Here's my in-a-nutshell, get-on-my-stump-and-preach sermon: I think that the church has fixated on sins of commission. "Don't do this. Don't do that." And the problem with that is you can do nothing right and still do nothing wrong. I think righteousness has more to do with those sins of omission. It's the things that we would've, could've, and should've done. I think the church has just been kind of blinded. We believe half the gospel in a sense, and honestly, it's a wonderful half of the gospel to know that my sins are forgiven. But it's not even the most exciting half. To me, the most exciting half is that other half where we're on mission and called into the plan that God has for us. So, that's kind of my overarching thought. This is one of the things that I try to preach to our congregation, because when you brought this topic up, Chris, it made me really think, *Oh man, do I have as full of an understanding of righteousness as I need to have?* You got me going on a little bit of a kick that I think is going to affect some of our servants coming up here.

I think 2 Corinthians 5:21 is a key verse to really help us understand this whole concept of sin: "God made him who had no sin to be sin for us, so that in him we might become the righteousness of God" [NIV]. It is not just about us transferring our sin to Christ's account. It's about Christ transferring his righteousness to our account. And without that full transfer, we're buying into a half-truth in a sense. That's my initial reflection on this topic.

CHRIS: I am so grateful for both of you. This helps a great deal.

SIX

Set Your Heart

Idolatry is really not good for anyone. Not even the idols.

— John Bach

I rode a motorcycle for a few years in college, and to be honest, I miss it. I know it is dangerous. I have four kids now, and very little money, and I live in a city where people believe the right of way is determined by the size of your car. So I am not likely to buy a new bike anytime soon. In fact, when my wife sees me perusing the classifieds and trolling Craigslist, she lovingly reminds me, "If you get injured on a bike, don't even ask me to care for you. If you can't feed yourself, get a nurse, because I won't lift a spoon." She really does love me, and the thought of the words "I told you so" rolling off her tongue easily dissuades me. Besides, my four-wheeled sedan runs on biodiesel, which means that I *must* love Jesus more than most people who drive huge gas guzzlers, right?

A friend gave me some riding advice years ago after I laid my motorcycle down in a deep pothole filled with gravel. He said, "You are driving in a way that you think is defensive—your eyes are scanning the road for obstacles, potholes, and dangerous objects. But by the time your eyes have identified a potential danger, you become fixated on it, and at that point it is too late to avoid it. You head straight for it—*crash*. Solution: Your bike will follow your eyes, so fix your eyes on the place you want to go and the bike will steer itself in that direction." I tried his advice, and it worked. Like Peter walking on water, we quickly learn that the direction of our focus is vital. Where have you set your gaze, love, affection, and self-worth? Is it found in God? The answer for most of us is, at best, "Sometimes."

Do you know anyone who thinks Christianity can be boiled down to ten big rules you must obey? Growing up in my dad's church, there was a saying: "We don't dip, drink, or chew, or kiss girls that do." So that was what they did. You have rules and you follow them. Then all of a sudden, Christianity becomes a religion, a behavior modification system, and behavior modification systems don't work. They are a futile waste of time. Who knows? Maybe you want to kiss girls who chew tobacco, though I don't know why you would. But I am also sure the Bible does not prohibit such behavior. At the end of the day, it just does not work. You don't believe me? Next January, make a New Year's resolution to lose fifteen pounds. That's one of the best ways on the planet to gain fifteen pounds. Why? Because simply willing yourself to do something is very different from actually doing it.

The first commandment (and the second as well) deals with issues of the heart, not behavior. The trouble is you can do the right thing, but if it's done for the wrong reasons, you are in more trouble than you'd be in for simply doing the wrong thing. I often sin, even when doing something deemed good by almost any standard. I may be serving the poor, preaching the gospel, or cleaning up after my children, but at times I do it for the approval of others, not God. Sometimes I even do things with or because of bitterness. My heart easily betrays me, and although it may take some time before my external actions reflect what is going on within me, clearly I have taken my eyes off of Jesus. The *what* I am doing is not my problem; my issue is *why* I am doing it. Essentially, I have broken the first commandment: *"First: you are to worship no other gods—My presence is enough, and as My people, you are always in My presence"* (Ex. 20:3).

I am convinced that these passages listing God's directives may be the most misunderstood in all of Scripture. You may be familiar with the Ten Commandments as the "ten things you are not supposed to do." The truth is they are nothing of the sort. Just as our forefathers found, if worshipping God is about modifying our behavior and straining to keep the rules, we will fail miserably. The root of idolatry within my heart will grow, apart from repentance, and will bring forth the fruit of death in my life. Idolatry changes our hearts long before it affects our actions. Donald Miller describes this struggle in his memoir *Blue Like Jazz*: "The problem is not out there; the problem is the needy beast of a thing that lives in my chest."[1] Or you may prefer the description offered by Sayid (a character on my favorite television show, *Lost*), describing the rabid fear of a black smoke monster that struck his fellow castaways: "I've worse things to fear than what's in the jungle. What I did today—what I almost did—I swore to do never again. If I can't keep that promise, I have no right to be here."[2]

When I was in eighth grade, my friend Chris and I were inseparable. We both got a bow and arrow (which was one of the coolest gifts ever for an eighth grader) and we'd shoot at targets behind his house. It was hard and took a long time to master. One day his mother did the unthinkable, laying down this rule: "Boys, you can shoot those targets, but there will be no flaming arrows." All of a sudden this became the coolest idea on earth, and it was instantly written in stone that we would do nothing else until we shot flaming arrows. If she wouldn't have mentioned the idea, we may never have thought of it. Instead, we almost burned down all of Atascocita, Texas—it was very stupid. (Kids, do not shoot flaming arrows . . . look, now I am the one preaching.) This is what rules can do to us.

Wicked behavior is not the problem. The root of idolatry is the problem that must be dealt with because we can do good things with wrong hearts and find ourselves lost in sin. We can leave church on Sunday and decide to feed the homeless—not because it is an outpouring of God's love, but because we think that is what we *should* do, and because we want to impress people. We may even try and work it into conversations the rest of the week to look great to the people around us. "When I was feeding the homeless in the rain last Sunday . . ." Sometimes we do good things just to look good to our peers, for prestige, to be liked . . . we do it for all the wrong reasons, but we find that even when we do what's right, we experience what the first commandment tells us is the source of all sin: idolatry.

This is a central understanding that we must teach as the church. If this foundational biblical truth is not understood, life will be spent running in circles, attempting to conform behavior. Let me save you the trouble now—it will not work. You can create a program intended to produce a specific outcome, and it may serve a great purpose (for example, providing people clean water, feeding the homeless, avoiding divorce, and so on), but do not be fooled. Although different from "Don't dip, kiss girls, etc.," this is still a system, and you can easily fall out of love with Jesus as you fixate on the new program that you have given your life to. We are not interested in a system. What we are interested in is God being at the center of our lives, and when God is in that place, he transforms everything we participate in. Our struggle is the tendency to put anything but God in that place. We want to be able to "act" out our salvation and "behave" our way into heaven. Behavior modification is not enough. You must deal with the fact that something or someone has become your functional god.

Can you recognize the idols in your life? If we truly understand the first commandment, then all things will start to fall into place. This is about having the life that God wants you to have. Martin Luther offers clues in *The Large Catechism* as he expounds on the meaning of the first commandment (that we shall have no other gods before God):

> That is: Thou shalt have [and worship] Me alone as thy God. What is the force of this, and how is it to be understood? What does it mean to have a god? Or, what is God?
>
> Answer: A god means that from which we are to expect all good and to which we are to take refuge in all distress, so that to have a God is nothing else than to trust and believe Him from the [whole] heart; as I have often said that the confidence and faith of the heart alone make both God and an idol. If your faith and trust be right, then is your god also true; and, on the other hand, if your trust be false and wrong, then you have not the true God; for these two belong together: faith and God. That now, I say, upon which you set your heart and put your trust is properly your god. [3]

These words are clear and insightful despite the fact that they were written five hundred years ago. Does this help you begin to see your own idols? What do you put your trust in? Said another way, what gives you purpose and what do you live for? What keeps you up at night, fearful that you might lose it or never attain it?

Jesus says, "Think of it this way: if your son asked you for bread, would you give him a stone? *Of course not—you would give him a loaf of bread"* (Matt. 7:9). A parent's instinct is to love, serve, and teach his or her children, but many parents cross over the line of loving their children and begin to worship them. Have you seen this happen? It sounds unselfish and big-hearted on one level that a parent would say, "I love you so much that I would do anything for you; I stay up at night worrying about the problems you might face and trying to protect you from illness or harm." But in reality, this is not good for the parent or the child. In this case, a healthy love swells and grows wildly into veneration, which leads to a narcissistic child and an obsessive parent. It may sound like a paradox, but the only way to love your child or your spouse well is to worship only God and simply love everyone else. A fine line can be crossed between loving something or someone and that love turning into obsession. We must trust God to care for those we love and rest in his ability to do what we cannot do. Our internal mirrors are curved, and our views are distorted. It is hard to find our bearings when our own wants (that new home, car, TV, girlfriend . . . you know what it is that comes to the forefront of your thoughts) are sabotaging our relationship with God. We cannot focus on him because of our obstructed view. Part of our faithful practice will be to walk around these things and step toward God. Although we may not see him clearly, he most certainly is there.

Idols can also be exposed through painful experiences, and by our disappointment and hatred. Have you ever been so consumed with resentment for someone else that your life began to revolve around the very person you despised? You buy things that might incite her to jealousy. You constantly compare yourself to him. Guess what? You have an idol. Is there a group of people you look down on? You judge them and feel justified; maybe they are liberals or legalists, but you judge them just the same. Has someone sinned against you and you are infuriated? Have you been burned? Paul says put it off, get rid of it, and let it go, because if you don't, anger will drive you. Your world will wrap around it, and the anger will come between you and God. Could anything be worse than finding out that your "worst enemy"—that jerk boss, the really fit aerobics instructor—is in fact your idol? Ouch. It hurts just thinking about it. People, whether they are friends, foes, or children, can easily become the things we center our lives around, and that is idolatry.

We live in an age of networking, which is often saying, "How can I use you?" We approach one another with our own agendas and wants. Paul wants us to wake up:

> So you can see there are no excuses for any of us. If your eyes shift their focus from yourselves to others—to judge *how they are doing*—you have already condemned yourselves! *You don't realize that* you are pointing your fingers at others for the exact things you do as well. The judgment of God will justly fall upon hypocrites who practice such things. *Here's what is happening*: you attack and criticize others and then turn around to commit the same offenses yourselves! Do you think you will somehow dodge God's judgment? Do you take the kindness of God for granted? Do you see His patience and tolerance as signs that He is a pushover *when it comes to sin?* How could you not know that His kindness is guiding our hearts to turn away from *distractions and habitual* sin to walk a new path?
>
> But because your heart is obstinate and shameless, you're storing up wrath that will count against you. On the day of His choosing, God's wrath and judgment will be unleashed to make things right. (Rom. 2:1–5)

Ed Clowney, a renowned seminary professor, concluded his teaching on the second chapter of Romans by saying, "It isn't legalism to try to glorify God in everything that we do. It isn't legalism to rejoice in the freedom that we have in Christ to live a new life."[4] Ed was right. When we cease to shine forth as people who seek first and foremost to glorify God, we have lost our way. We serve that which we set our hearts upon; whatever you love most owns you. That is what is so beautiful about making Jesus your Lord and King. He takes the throne of your life, but he does not seek to dominate and rule over us; he came to liberate us. As we move under the reign of God, we are truly free for the first time. It may sound like a paradox, but it is not.

Idols are self-justification projects. We believe that if we get the desires of our hearts (the idols), they will fulfill us, making the world right again. We hear in Exodus 20 that the people had fabricated an idol, a golden calf, and it's easy to think that these people were idiots for worshipping a statue. We can mock them for their grumbling, and call them dumb, but I imagine them in heaven right now having a clear view of our hearts. They know everything we buy, why we buy, and how it all makes us feel. They know we shop because it promises us happiness or fulfillment, whether it's buying a new car, a toaster, or a little wine cellar to put your wine in. We really believe, *When I get that, I will be happy*. And for a few moments it is bliss. But bliss doesn't last long, does it? The car drives you for a while, but you never hear an advertisement saying, "This is the last car you will ever buy." Eventually the first monthly payment arrives, the thrill dies, and you are out looking for another god (and another god, and another). You may disagree that these things are gods, but if you find something besides God at the center of your world, that is a warning sign.

These people are not ignorant about what can be known of God, because He has shown it to them *with great clarity*. From the beginning the magnitude of creation enlightens us to His invisible nature. Creation itself makes His undying power and divine identity clear and voids the *ignorant claims* of these people because, despite the fact that they knew the one true God, they have failed to show the *love*, honor, and appreciation due to the One who created them! Instead, their lives are consumed by vain thoughts that poison their foolish hearts. They claim to be wise, but they have been exposed as fools, *frauds, and con-artists*—only a fool would trade the splendor and beauty of the immortal God to worship images of the common man or woman, bird or reptile, or *the next* beast *that tromps along.*

So God gave them just what their lustful hearts desired. *As a result* they violated their bodies and invited shame into their lives. *How?* By choosing a foolish lie over God's truth. They gave their lives and devotion to the creature rather than to the Creator Himself, who is blessed forever and ever. Amen. (Rom. 1:19–25)

And beasts *will* tromp along. The next new thing, the next friendship, a diamond ring, a new baby . . . The best thing you can do for your life, your kids, your marriage, and your city is to put Jesus in the center of your life. Do everything in the name of Jesus. If you take Jesus out of Christianity, you will have nothing but a set of rules, laws, and empty restrictions. You will be like kids with flaming arrows, wondering how big the flames are going to be. There is nothing we (or any person outside of Jesus) can do to change us. So what do we focus on? Jesus. Jesus changes our hearts, and without heart change, behavior change is meaningless. We will fail. I hope for our sake we learn along the way, because failing is painful. The proof of our faith is not in willing ourselves to do the right thing; it is in allowing Jesus to capture our hearts. And when he does, we root out the other things so our hearts can sing.

The most important prayer in the life of a devout Jew is the *Shema*, which Jesus introduces to us in Mark 12.

> Jesus: The most important commandment is this: "Hear, O Israel, the Eternal One is our God, and the Eternal One is the only God. You should love the Eternal, your God, with all your heart, with all your soul, with all your mind, and with all your strength." (vv. 29–30)

Remember, God's movement toward us has been completed in Jesus.

You see, God takes all our crimes—our seemingly inexhaustible sins—and removes them. As far as east is from the west, He removes them from us (Ps. 103:12).

We often try to make a life of faith very complicated. But in the end it is as simple as "love God and do as you wish." As we seek out the righteousness of God rather than our own vain pursuit to make things right, pray with me the *Shema*.

PRAYER

Hear, O Israel, the Lord is our God; the Lord is One. Blessed is His name, whose glorious kingdom is forever and ever. Love the Lord your God with all your heart, and all your soul, and all your might. These words that I command you today shall be upon your heart. Repeat them to your children, and talk about them when you sit in your home, and when you walk in the street; when you lie down, and when you rise up. Hold fast to them as a sign upon your hand, and let them be as reminders before your eyes. Write them on the doorposts of your home and at your gates. (Deut. 6:4–9, paraphrase)

Interview with Rick McKinley and Shane Claiborne

Rick and Shane live on opposite coasts in neighborhoods that are radically divergent, but they share a passion for relationships and a healthy understanding of the destructive power of sin. This conversation will enlighten your understanding no matter where you live.

CHRIS: Rick, can you give me your observation on the word *righteousness*? This Hebrew and Greek word comes up repeatedly among the prophets. Jesus talks about it; Paul talks a lot about it in Romans. Do you think we're potentially misreading the meaning of it, and if so, what are the effects on the church?

RICK: Well, I think the massive effect is we don't really understand the gospel, what Christ actually accomplished for us; therefore it becomes an identity issue, both individually and corporately.

CHRIS: Based on the responses that most people gave for how they understand righteousness, how would you compare that to what Jesus talks about as the righteousness of the Pharisees?

RICK: It feels like there's a lot of confusion, and a tendency to talk about righteousness from a purely moral standpoint as opposed to perhaps the larger picture the Scriptures are talking about. You can see that the tension comes in when we try to define *righteousness* as "doing the right thing"— pleasing God, reading the Word of God, those kinds of answers—as opposed to viewing it through the relational lens that actually brings me into relationship with Christ. So the sense of religious duty goes way up. And relationship, longing, desire—those things go way down. I think the implicit confusion within the believer comes when he thinks, *Christ died on the cross to forgive me, and now I need to get my crap together.*

CHRIS: Paul makes this really clear that a gift is a gift. So there's no beating around the bush in the Scriptures. Yet somehow we still have a tendency to try to attach some kind of works to our salvation, which most often has been that

The Dealing with Dead Faith

"The church is the answer to this crisis, and though she is struggling to
find her voice in this fractured world, she is no less the bride of Christ,
beloved by Jesus the King. Somewhere along the way, she has lost the
sense of awe and wonder of her salvation. But what is lost can be
restored." (p. 4)

The Kingdom of Heaven Is Like

"This is the beauty God has called us to participate in. Not a life of perfection but a journey. One that will send us all the way to the gates of hell and allow us to see God redeem all things and make all things right. This is not a stale, mind-numbing religious existence. This is a quest into the depths of darkness to shine the light of life and join God's transforming work in this beautifully broken world." (pg. 33)

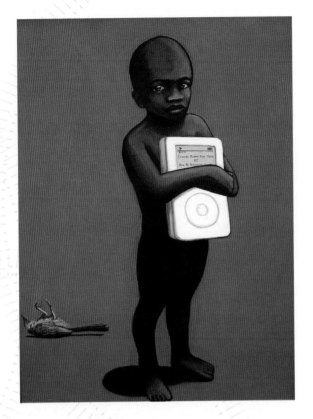

The Value of $300

"My love for the poor will ebb and flow, and my commitment to do the right thing is fleeting. It is my response to the radical love and grace of Jesus the Liberating King that has the power to change the world. It is only when I live as one rescued that I see the source of salvation is not by the work of my own hands. A social gospel is not the gospel any more than a spiritual gospel is the gospel." (pg. 23)

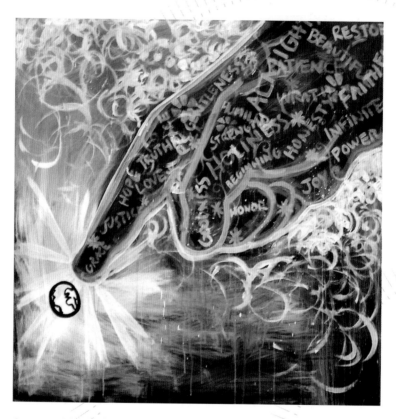

Image of God

"Genesis certainly calls humans to be collaborators with God in his redemptive work that is reshaping the cosmos according to his will. He has created all that exists, and now he invites us to work with our own entrusted creative gifts to bring about his glory as this narrative continues to unfold, one creative, permitted breath at a time." (pg. 70)

We Don't Need You

"Jesus steps in, and in his presence says, "I am here to restore what has been broken—the imago dei that is shattered. I'll enter and I'll begin to put the pieces together." Through his saving act, he is gathering us up into himself. . . . we begin to reflect the beauty of God once again. The divine spark does not come from within us; we reflect into the world the character and the nature of God as it shines upon us, through us, and off us." (pp. 75–76)

Rise

"The truth is that the resurrection of Jesus initiates a journey intended to bring shalom to all of creation. That includes our broken hearts, our broken relationships, our broken cities, and those living in extreme poverty across the globe." (pp. 163–64)

YA Community

"We desperately need to be part of communities where fences are being torn down, where we're drawn together with people who aren't like us, where we are willing to learn from one another, where beautiful things begin to happen." (pg. 183)

Forgive Thy Brother

"Jesus' people are not perfect. They are broken, they will disappoint you, but they will also inspire you. They will fail you, but they will also love you. If you love Jesus and want to be part of Jesus' reign, it also means that you are part of Jesus' (broken) people. Welcome to the family." (pg. 27)

kind of religious ritual that Jesus is talking about with the Pharisees and seems to be the one thing he's most clearly opposing.

RICK: Paul talks about "unless your righteousness surpasses that [of the] Pharisees," and these are guys who worked really hard to keep the law. So if you are looking for the morally elite, Paul would say, "I was one of those people. I was a Hebrew of Hebrews, a Pharisee of Pharisees. Except when it came to this one particular sin of coveting—then I found myself unable to keep the law." The law is revealed to enhance sin and to show that I can't keep it. That's why it's so ridiculous when you tag righteousness into moral duty, because if it's just human effort, you're never going to be able to fulfill it. It has to be something bigger than that. Otherwise, you are saying that we are forgiven by Christ but we come to Jesus through our own effort.

CHRIS: Shane, do you think we fully grasp the beauty of forgiveness? Why is it so hard to live a life marked by grace?

SHANE: I think one of the things that we have to start with is a healthy understanding of what sin is. A lot of the conversation around the pious and the puritanical kind of righteousness is, I think, rooted in this idea that God hates sin. I think the question we have to begin with is, why does God hate sin? God doesn't hate sin because we're breaking some random rules. God hates sin because it destroys us and because God can't stand to watch us destroy ourselves and other people. I think that is really critical to understand because otherwise we make a monster out of God, as if God is just a policeman waiting for us to break the rules and smite us. But God is love. When we sin we fall short of what love requires of us, and that's exactly what justice is about. It's about doing what love requires of us; it's about not looking at women in a way that destroys their dignity and the image of God in them; it's about divorce being a terrible idea not just because it's against God's law, but because it rips people apart.

CHRIS: Are you concerned that our tendency may be to minimize sin?

SHANE: The idea that God hates sin because God is love is really fundamental to understanding how righteousness and justice come together. When it comes to morality, Jesus' story about the tax collector and the Pharisee who goes to pray is a great story because it shows us that God didn't come to make bad people good, but to bring dead people alive. You can be moral but not alive. And maybe the Pharisee did keep up the law and all the rules—unlikely as it may be—but even if he was moral and alive, living a socially conscious lifestyle, and buying all fair-trade products, he might have still been mean and judgmental. If we don't give life to other people, then it's a pretty good litmus test that it's not the Spirit working in us, because the Spirit brings goodness, gentleness, patience, and kindness.

Many righteous people I've met don't seem to reflect the

traits of the Spirit; that is the real litmus test of the Spirit living in us. Will kindness come out of us? Patience? Patience with people that are struggling with their own brokenness? So Jesus says to the Pharisee that the tax collectors and prostitutes are entering the kingdom ahead of you—because they still have the humility to beat their chests and ask for forgiveness. The problem with self-righteousness is we often find that we can't beat our chests; we have to act like we have it all together. The great tragedy within the church is that we've flipped this around, believing Jesus came for the healthy instead of the sick, although it's the exact opposite. Jesus came for wounded people who were broken and had the humility to not even lift their heads to heaven but beat their chests and say, "God, I need help." That is what this gospel is about—we're all hypocrites, and there is always room for one more.

In light of this, it's really important for those of us who grew up with a legalistic background to not have a knee-jerk reaction to it, saying, "So we're just going to create a safe place for everybody and not tell each other how to live—to find this murky liberalism that perpetuates brokenness so that we don't end up seeing healing and wholeness." We have to be very careful. I see a lot of communities and church plants and things like that being radically inclusive—which I think is a beautiful part of Jesus—but also we have to be radically disciplined, because *disciple* shares the same word as *discipline*.

I saw an interview with a social psychology parenting guru who pioneered the hands-off parenting that taught parents to let their kids makes mistakes and learn on their own. They asked him, "What have you learned from this?" And he said, "Well, it all looked good on paper"—his idea challenged discipline-oriented parenting—"but we've created a generation of brats." I thought that was so powerful because in the church we are in danger of creating a generation of brats by reacting in this shallow and maladjusted view of righteousness. We end up running the other direction with a really sloppy spirituality, or as Dietrich Bonhoeffer called it, "cheap grace," wherein love doesn't require something of us.

I wrote a piece called "When Jesus and Justice Kiss," and it's on the God's Politics Blog [www.godspolitics.com]. One of the things I said in the piece that I think is really true, and what you're finding out through this book, is that part of what we do in church is to overcorrect ourselves so that we exaggerate the truth. The truth is neglected to the point that we get really imbalanced with our faith. We end up making Jesus disciples who don't really talk about justice because the social-gospel people did it wrong or something. And we end up having Jesus disciples who aren't about justice, or we end up having justice disciples who aren't about Jesus, and that really leaves us with a lopsided Christianity that falls short of Jesus' true gospel.

SEVEN

Justification: Rise or Fall?

It means nothing to be open to a proposition we don't understand.

— Carl Sagan

Do you remember the first life-threatening crisis faced by the crew of *Apollo 13*? A little more than two days into their 1970 voyage to the moon, a cryogenic oxygen tank exploded onboard the shuttle, which caused a loss of power, damage to the craft, and endangered the lives of the three astronauts aboard as their oxygen supply quickly plummeted. The 1995 movie directed by Ron Howard brought this life-or-death encounter out of distant space and into our living rooms. Imagine the tension of being in outer space, where you can't just open a window for some fresh air.

We may think we do a good job of planning out our daily calendars, but we can't even imagine what goes into planning the day-to-day living of people traveling in space. Air, food, water, waste . . . you name it, it has to be accounted for. So with carbon monoxide building and oxygen depleting, the crew of *Apollo 13* moved into the lunar module, the vehicle they had planned to use for breathable air during their planned moon landing. But it was only built for two, so with a third person in the ultimate all-terrain vehicle, clean oxygen was still a concern. The geniuses that engineer the space program gathered to solve the problem. They had to fix the craft and get the crew home safely with whatever "ingredients" the ship contained. They raided small pieces from many parts of the ship, added some packing material, stuck it all together with some ever-useful duct tape, and managed to rig together some lithium hydroxide canisters (translate: space air filters) made with square ends for the main ship to fit into the round ends of the lunar module's system. (I wonder if they all have the same ends these days?) Problem solved, air breathed, astronauts safely home.[1]

Ever wonder how history might have been different if there had been no duct tape on board, or the engineers lacked the commitment or creativity to find the solution? The problem was potentially fatal. The solution was creative, and the result rescued the mission. If there is a mission control–type center somewhere in heaven, we can imagine that there is some wringing of hands over the way the church is drifting in space. The church that does not grasp a theology of justification is aimlessly falling (according to Martin Luther), and it seems the church of the twenty-first century is plummeting into a historic debacle on many fronts. Jesus is the great hope of the world, but in our pursuit of religious rigor, rather than the biblical understanding of righteousness, we have asked the world to serve the church.

We have invited the masses to become the older brother in Luke 15: do your duty, pay your tithes, come to church, be respectable, and carry your Bible with you as you go. Seems doable, and it is. It is also the wide road that leads to destruction, specifically a spiritual pride that will lead to a calamitous fall. The narrow path will require us to join God in his redemptive work to restore the world and return it to its rightful state: paradise, heaven on earth, the kingdom of God, the reign of King Jesus. It doesn't matter what you call it, but this path calls the church to be the unified body that manifests the presence of Christ as we redeem, forgive, heal, wash the feet of, die for, and serve the world.

The purpose of this book is not to merely inform a correct and proper understanding of justification (the doctrine founded on the biblical teaching of righteousness). We have a problem, and we must look again at the teachings of Jesus and seek the truth with our lives. Correcting our misguided assumptions is meaningless if we do not hold this truth in the forefront of our hearts, minds, and lives. As always, Jesus said it best:

> Not everyone who says to Me, "Lord, Lord," will enter the kingdom of heaven. *Simply calling Me "Lord" when you reach heaven will not be enough.* Only those who do the will of My Father who is in heaven *will join Me in heaven.* (Matt.7:21)

It seems that knowing the facts is not enough. Good doctrine is of no value if it is tucked away in a dusty library. Our God was (and is) moved to action. He is a triune God who lives in a constant state of motion.

A Grandparent in the Sky

When you pray, how do you picture God? Very few people imagine a fast-moving deity who pursues his prize at a pace much faster than the Jamaican sprinter Hussein Bolt. Most think of an elderly grandparent whose only motion is the gentle rocking of a chair, maybe giving a pat on the head, or a look of disappointment. That is not the God of the Bible; we worship a God in motion who pursues all of us in the midst of our sin and seeks to restore all that is broken. He meets us in all his power in every moment. With this gift of power, he calls us to join in his restorative work, redeeming all of creation and reestablishing his Garden (we know it as the kingdom of God).

Our doctrine, when properly aligned, will not only connect us to the truth that Jesus taught; it will alter our pace to sync up with the movement of the Holy Spirit and will redefine our mission and purpose here on earth. As you and I share in the experience of this book, I pray the Holy Spirit mends the gaps of our incomplete theology. That we gain an understanding of how it is that we are justified, and what it means to seek the kingdom and his righteousness. Our success in connecting with the gospel according to Jesus cannot be measured in a written theological exam, but will be demonstrated instead by a life lived in relationship to a triune God who actively restores relationships among all of his creations.

There is great consensus about the importance of the subject matter for this book among theologians, pastors, educators, and authors throughout history. The Reformation was founded on the need for the church to recapture a biblical understanding of righteousness. It is both ironic and sad that five hundred years later only 38 percent of Christians who identify with reformed traditions say they are very familiar with the concept of righteousness. A writer and founder of a Puritan Web site, Dr. C. Matthew McMahon, put it this way:

There may be a doctrine, which is more important than any other; one, which is the most important of all . . . Today, I believe, as it was in the sixteenth century, the need to regain lost ground in understanding the doctrine of justification by faith alone has come to the forefront. Most people, even those in reformed circles, those who claim Luther as a hero, have little to say about justification. I have been a member of solid reformed churches for quite a long time. Yet, I have heard very little about justification by faith alone. I cannot remember a sermon dedicated to the subject. It has been neglected in the school setting, in the home study groups, and in the pulpit. It is a vital doctrine that we cannot do without.[2]

The fact that so many people who claim to be followers of Jesus are ignorant about justification through faith and who often pursue a set of rules instead of real Christianity grieves me deeply. I would not want anyone in my congregation to be ignorant on any issue of faith. But if I were to prioritize their areas of study, the doctrine of justification by faith would undoubtedly top the list. I stand with the reformers and generations of church leaders who have passionately taught this doctrine. If we are justified, or made right, in any way other than faith in Jesus alone, we have arrived at a different gospel. John MacArthur says it this way: "No doctrine is more important to evangelical theology than the doctrine of justification by faith alone—the Reformation principle of *sola fide*. Martin Luther called it the article that determines whether the church is standing or falling."[3]

We are becoming aware that the majority of Christians are not even capable of articulating a definition for righteousness, so we can be quite sure that very few are able to take the next step and portray a robust doctrine of justification. If Luther's words are true, the church is not standing strong; we are falling away aimlessly. It is time we explore the theology and key passages in the Bible that speak of righteousness. Let's enter into this five-hundred-year-old conversation. I will give you some things to think about, pull insights from Scripture, and encourage you to reflect on your own life. Ultimately this must be a work of the Holy Spirit, who guides us to sound doctrine and inspires us to Christian action.

> God did something the law could never do. *You see, human flesh took its toll on God's law. In and of itself the law is not weak; but* the flesh weakens it. So to condemn the sin that was ruling in the flesh, God sent His own Son, bearing the likeness of sinful flesh, as a sin offering. Now we are able to live up to the justice demanded by the law. But that ability has not come from living by our fallen human nature; it has come because we walk according to the movement of the Spirit in our lives. (Rom. 8:3–4)

From this passage it is clear that we are freed with a purpose: to accomplish his restorative justice. It is accomplished through Jesus, not the law. So, will you tune in to what God is saying to you and think carefully about this subject?

The word *diak* or *tsedk* (righteousness) may seem like just another word in the Bible, but to theologians an essential doctrine has been formed around this single word. We call it the doctrine of justification, and it is of great importance. Defining this doctrine well is not easy; but while the core of our understanding usually brings wide agreement, other areas inspire intense dialogue and disagreement among theologians and Bible scholars. The temptation is to dismiss this theological inquiry as an exercise for scholars, but it is a practical and indispensable truth for all who place their faith in Jesus.

In fact, the Reformation became a reality primarily because of Martin Luther's concern that the church (in fact, the ruling pope) was teaching sinners that certain actions were required on the part of the sinner (for example, indulgences) to receive absolution of sin. Not everyone understood what the reformers were so worked up about. They probably thought, *So what if they need to chip a little extra money in the church coffers when they sin? Not only does the sinner feel better, but it also helps the church build some beautiful cathedrals. It is a fair price for the fun of sinning.* Even today, many in our church might favor a do-it-yourself system—if you sin, then you pay the fine.

The practice of indulgences inside the Catholic Church has long since vanished, but the same tendency or desire to work off our sins is alive and well. Some teach that baptism or signing a particular faith statement or even tithing is required for salvation. One could advance a similar argument today: "What's the big deal if the church requires you to be baptized, tithe, or, say, demand that every believer support an orphanage?" Think about it. If the church required every believer to sponsor a child, the world would be a better place; every child would be well fed, educated, and cared for when they are sick. Who in their right mind could be against requiring that? Jesus. It seems that he has no desire to force us to do anything.

Jesus + Anything ≠ Christian Salvation

The Scriptures are clear that a person can be justified by faith alone. There is nothing anyone can do to earn the freedom Jesus gifted. Paul explains this in Romans:

> Now, when you work a job, does your paycheck come to you as a gift *or as compensation for your work?* It is *most certainly* not a gift—you are only paid what you have earned. So for the person who does not work, but instead trusts in the One who makes the ungodly right, his faith is counted for him as righteousness. (4:4–5)

Just think of it this way: There is no half gift. Something is either a gift or a wage; there is no in between. When you get a gift that has strings attached to it, it is *not* a gift. Have you ever fallen for, I mean, attended one of those timeshare tours that promise an amazing gift?

What happens if you leave halfway into the daylong meeting? Do you get the gift? No. And, if you stayed, did the big prize feel like a gift? When I attended one of those meetings, I felt like I was paid, that I earned that microwave and free night stay by walking around the better part of a day, sipping stale coffee, nodding my head, and then waxing eloquent in my refusal to buy in. We often treat matters of faith like one of these manipulative seminars filled with guilt, obligation, and a high-pressure sales pitch. It is nothing of the sort.

If we have to work or give money or circumcise our sons or be charitable to the poor to earn salvation, then the gospel according to Jesus is not present. As Paul says, if that is the case, then the sacrifice of Jesus was the greatest waste of all time. Salvation is a gift, 100 percent through and through. Many churches have gone astray by losing sight of this simple truth. One of these churches was in Galatia, and Paul did not mince words in condemning their deviation from the true faith.

Frankly, I am stunned. I cannot believe that you have abandoned God so quickly—even after He called you through the grace of the Liberating King—and have fallen for a different gospel. Actually, there is only one true gospel, and you—because of divisive prodding by others—are accepting a distorted version of the Liberator's promise, which is not the gospel at all! *People are deceiving you with some cut-up imitation of the true gospel, and you have bought into it. Their words are nothing but twisted lies.* No matter the source of the false gospel, even if it is preached by us or a heavenly messenger, *ignore it.* May those *who add to or subtract from the gospel of Jesus be eternally* cursed! Listen again *because I am going to make it crystal clear*: if anyone preaches to you a gospel other than what you have accepted, may he find himself cursed! *Take this message for what it is: a truthful warning.* (Gal. 1:6–9)

Paul might as well be speaking to us today. The air that we breathe is consumerism. It pervades everything we do. So it is understandable that when we take our eyes off of Jesus and begin to drift, we will float away from the gospel according to Jesus toward a consumer gospel, which is, as Paul says, "no gospel at all." We try to make a deal with Jesus. "I'll do this in exchange for forgiveness and that eternal life thing." But salvation does not come with a mortgage leveraged against our soul that will threaten foreclosure if the payments don't arrive. It comes to us with a clear title. And that is truly amazing; in fact, that is why we call it amazing grace.

In 2008, as Hurricane Ike threatened certain destruction of Galveston, Texas, and despite an official evacuation order, three individuals (one engaged couple and a friend) decided to ride out the storm in a small building attached to a pier that juts out from the Galveston Seawall. The three imagined it was a safe place because it was built of steel and concrete and had previously survived two intense storms. Moments after the three decided to head upstairs from the bait shop/restaurant to watch TV in the apartment on the second floor, wave surges totally destroyed the first floor of the building. Washed it completely away. Waves swayed the structure from side to side and threw it up and down for hours, even causing the furniture to slam into the ceiling and fall back to the ground.

The next morning, as the structure was teetering, they called 911 and were rescued by a Coast Guard helicopter that, ironically, fished them off the pier with a long rope baited with a hero and a basket. One man said that it was the scariest experience of his life, but he always believed they would make it. What would we give to be rescued from our bad choices? To be saved from every mistake we have made? This trio is a living example of the marvel of salvation. Can you imagine their relief when they saw that line lowered? Have you ever felt desperation melt into relief in your whole being?

Can you imagine the gratitude you would feel every time you saw a Coast Guard helicopter fly over the Gulf Coast beaches?

Three people made a series of very stupid choices; they ignored the warnings and the mandated evacuation. You would think they would be apologetic and grateful beyond words for their rescue. But what if they had scoffed at their rescuers and complained that they had not come sooner? "We waited all night in the cold and darkness for you to come!" Can you imagine them grumbling about anything as they were lifted to safety? What if they felt entitled and did not even bother to thank the men and women who risked their lives to rescue them? Imagine that same trio watching the next hurricane hit, apathetic about others in need of rescue. It seems absurd, doesn't it? But that is often the mind-set of many Christians about the much greater gift of salvation through faith in Jesus. If we properly understand justification, we could never take our salvation for granted or look down on another "wretch like me," no matter how ugly his or her sins might be to us. We have been freed from the chains of sin and death; God has led us, like the children of Israel, out of slavery, and is guiding us to the land of abundance. No matter how you spin it, that is a gift we have not earned and do not deserve. So Paul made his case without apology: if you have been freed, do not choose to place yourself back in the chains; instead, celebrate your freedom in the Liberating King.

So stand strong for our freedom! The Liberating King freed us so we wouldn't spend one more day under the yoke of slavery; *don't let anyone get you turned around and trapped under the law.*

Listen because I, Paul, am going to make this message very clear *so it cannot be misunderstood:* if you undergo the rite of circumcision, then all that the Liberating King accomplished will be lost on you. And understand this: if you choose to be circumcised, then you will oblige yourself to do every single rule of the law *for the rest of your life.* You, *and anyone else* who seeks to be on the right side of God through the law, have effectively been cut off from the Liberator, *circumcised from grace,* and cast off from the favor of God—*the favor that could have set you free.* We, on the other hand, *continue to live* through the Spirit's power and wait confidently in the hope that things will be put right through faith. Here's the thing: in Jesus the Liberator, whether you are circumcised or not makes no difference. What makes a difference is faith energized by love. (Gal. 5:1–6)

We have been restored, renewed, declared righteous, and justified by Jesus alone. The Scriptures then call us in that completed state to love as we have been loved and forgive as we have been forgiven. In other words, to show justice to others in the same way it has been shown to us: "Instead, be kind and compassionate. *Graciously* forgive one another just as God has forgiven you through the Liberating King" (Eph. 4:32).

Defining Righteousness

The righteousness of Jesus the Liberating King is the means of our salvation and not our own works; so how are we to define this righteousness? If we carefully read these passages, it will not only reshape our doctrine; it will transform our actions. Luther described justification by faith as "the Sun which illuminates God's Church." If you and I meditate on the meaning of this doctrine, we will begin to see all things anew. We will see God's grace showing up in the most unexpected places. In the words of N. T. Wright:

The doctrine of justification comes into play because the whole plan of God is and has been right since the Fall to sort out the mess that the world is in. We British say, "to put the world to rights." I've discovered that that's not the way Americans say it and people scratch their heads and say, "Funny . . . what does he mean by that?" It means to fix the thing, to make it all better again.[4]

The catastrophic fallout of sin is being set right by the righteousness of God. We can reason from this definition that God intends to use the church as the means to set things right. John Howard Yoder defines it this way:

> We could in fact most properly say that the word "justification" . . . should be thought of in its roots meaning, as a verbal noun, an action, "setting things right," rather than as an abstract noun defining a person's quasi-legal status as a result of a judge's decree. To proclaim divine righteousness means to proclaim that God sets things right; it is characteristic of the God who makes a covenant with us to be a right-setting kind of God.[5]

I define *justification* this way: "God's restorative justice." Because God is working on all levels at once in a way that human beings cannot fully grasp, we must attempt to understand righteousness on two planes:

1) Cosmically—God is making all relationships right, restoring his creation that is broken with his divine justice.
2) Personally—The justice of God declares his glory and brings about our own justification in Christ (by grace and through faith alone). In order to make things right (for a fallen sinful human), God imputes his character upon us as he bore the weight of our sin.

God's restorative justice is moving in unison. One aspect cannot be pitted against the other, but must be seen as an integrated expression of the character of the triune God.

Saved for a Purpose?

If the righteousness of God is intended to make things right on a cosmic level, then why is the world such a mess? Because the arm of God's redemptive work is ignorant when it comes to justification and righteousness and thus, in Luther's words, the church is falling. How far have we fallen? Our failure can be seen in its fullness when we examine brokenness on a global scale. As we entered the twenty-first century, nearly a billion people were unable to read a book or sign their names.[6] We may be waiting for a scientific breakthrough to cure cancer or finally eradicate AIDS from the planet, but we are able to teach the illiterate and educate the masses. Our greatest failures cannot be blamed on our resources or capacity, only our wills.

Infectious diseases continue to blight the lives of the poor across the world. An estimated 40 million people are living with HIV/AIDS, with 3 million deaths in 2004. Every year there are 350–500 million cases of malaria, with 1 million fatalities: Africa accounts for 90 percent of malarial deaths, and African children account for more than 80 percent of malaria victims worldwide.[7]

More than 24,000 children die every day around the world. That is equivalent to:

- 1 child dying every 3.6 seconds
- 16–17 children dying every minute
- a 2010 Haitian earthquake occurring almost every 9–10 days

- a 2004 Asian tsunami occurring almost every 10 days
- an Iraq-scale death toll every 16–40 days
- just under 9 million children dying every year
- some 79 million children dying between 2000 and 2007

The silent killers are poverty, hunger, easily preventable diseases and illnesses, and other related causes. In spite of the scale of this daily, ongoing catastrophe, it rarely manages to achieve, much less sustain, prime-time, headline coverage.[8]

And as it all unfolds, churches in America are embarking on yet another sermon series about success, happiness, and a sense of personal fulfillment. The problem was never clearer to me than during a recent visit to a small church in my city. Given the saturation of technology in our culture, it should not have surprised me to find seven flat-screen television sets mounted in a church. What surprised me is that the seven sets were mounted in one men's bathroom. As I stood over a urinal where announcements and videos are constantly replayed to those seeking simply to empty their bladder, I remembered a conversation with a village woman in Liberia. I naively asked this woman, who was standing by a river, where children were both gathering water and bathing, how many children had died in their village from unsafe drinking water. This young mother started to count, and it was clear that there were more children than she was capable of counting. Finally she answered simply, "By me, three." This dear woman lost three of her own children to cholera (due to drinking river water) in one year. She was dumbfounded to hear that we flush our toilets in the United States with clean drinking water. How could we waste such a precious commodity like clean water when it meant the difference between life and death for her children? Her bewilderment at our wastefulness brought home the reality of our failure, and as I stood in this church restroom, I wondered what she would think of us if she could see this display of senseless wealth.

It is estimated that there are between 143 million and 210 million orphans worldwide.[9] To give you an idea of the enormity of those numbers, the current population of the United States is just a little over 300 million, and the current population of Russia is 141 million. Every day 5,760 more children become orphans, and 2,102,400 more children become orphans every year in Africa alone. Every 15 seconds, another child in Africa becomes an AIDS orphan. There are an estimated 14 million AIDS orphans in sub-Saharan Africa (a number higher than the total of every under-eighteen-year-old in Canada, Norway, Sweden, Denmark, and Ireland combined). According to a 2007 tally, this figure is estimated to reach 18 million orphans in Africa alone in 2010. Eight out of 10 children orphaned by AIDS live in sub-Saharan Africa. Approximately 250,000 children are adopted annually, but . . . each year 14,505,000 children grow up as orphans and age out of the system by age sixteen. Each day 38,493 orphans age out. Every 2.2 seconds another orphan ages out with no family to belong to and no place to call home.

In Russia and the Ukraine, studies have shown that 10 to 15 percent of these children commit suicide before they reach the age of eighteen. These studies also show that 60 percent of the girls become prostitutes and 70 percent of the boys become hardened criminals. Another Russian study reported that of the 15,000 orphans aging out of state-run institutions every year, 10 percent committed suicide, 5,000 were unemployed, 6,000 were homeless, and 3,000 were in prison within three years.[10]

The world is deeply broken, but a church in action can solve these plights. May shalom come.

PRAYER

God, we see all too clearly the fruit of our ignorance. We long to be your unblemished bride who joins in your divine work to make all things right. Guide us out of apathy, ignorance, and paralyzed fear and into your kingdom. We want to do much more than cry out to you as Lord; we want to do your will here on earth. Help us to see our faith (and often lack of faith) as clearly as the Liberian woman who was so disappointed at our failure to share our leftovers. Your grace comes to us freely, but it calls us to join you in suffering as an expression of your love to all of creation. May the church experience the power of another world-changing reformation that centers our lives on salvation through faith alone.

Interview with Alan Hirsch, Dan Kimball, and Mark Batterson

If you began reading this book with very little understanding of the important theological terms we have been studying, do not despair. Dan Kimball says that he (as many others) made it through seminary without actually studying the word *righteousness*. If Alan is right, we need to take time to study many other key terms as well.

CHRIS: It is a bit scary and somewhat remarkable when we begin to realize how many pastors and seminary graduates often lack a basic understanding of justice or righteousness. Have you noticed other areas where we often lack understanding?

ALAN: I guess the same idea relates to the idea of holiness. If you ask most people what holiness is, they would have very moralistic perspectives on it, and I think it is somewhat of a distortion of what the Bible means. It includes the moral, but it's way beyond that.

CHRIS: We seem to be attempting to define Christianity in a way that feels manageable—keep the rules, go to church, do the right thing—but the cosmic work of God is so much bigger and more beautiful than that. We grew up in church, we examine every Greek word, and yet we get to the climax of Jesus' teaching at the Sermon on the Mount and we miss the point. I grew up thinking that the kingdom of God was heaven and you're just supposed to get saved so you can go to heaven, and that righteousness was just about moral religious pursuit, and neither of those things is true. It makes you realize how far off the path we have gotten. As people who have spent so much time examining exact words in the Bible, how do we miss the mark by so much?

ALAN: It's curious because the same thing is happening with our idea of holiness. Somehow we have interpreted the big ideas of the faith, including justification, which relates very much to this concept of righteousness, through a somewhat religious lens in our self-righteousness, and it's the very sort of thing the Bible is trying to work against. We've become people who assume we can pull it off ourselves and that righteousness is within our power rather than a gift that God gives us, and therefore we can live consistently in righteousness. I think it goes back to the issue of religion. I think religion always distorts the faith; I think it always brings it down to a controllable proportion so that we can make it something that we can handle, something within our power, rather than letting it call us to change. We get religious and like to have it our way.

CHRIS: Talk a little bit about your perspective on the reformed view of righteousness. For Luther this is really important. He said, "The churches are rising or falling based on our understanding of this theology," and yet reform churches have almost lost much of that sense, and have tried to come back to the ways that we do it ourselves. In the Old Testament, Isaiah says the fruit of righteousness is shalom. How do you see in that Hebrew perspective—the connection between righteousness (as we translate it, "restorative justice") and shalom?

ALAN: The main way I see it in Scriptures is that *righteousness* calls us to be in right relationship with God, with other human beings, and with the earth. It's a strongly relational term, I think. From the core of Old Testament teachings particularly, it's not primarily a legal term, although it takes juridical-legal tones in the Prophets. Luther picked up on this and developed it into the doctrine we know so well. But the primary matrix I think remains relational. Luther is therefore right, but he emphasizes the one over against the other. I think of it more in terms of both/and. Another thing is that, for Luther, it becomes the organizing center of the gospel, and I am not sure this is right. It was certainly the right message for his day—people were dealing more with a great sense of guilt before God, and I think that justification as Luther articulated it is the completely appropriate gospel response. I think that has always been the gospel, but the problem is that our sense of sin (or the problem itself) has shifted. I don't think that guilt before God is what most people are dealing with now. They be might feeling a great sense of shame (comes with promiscuity) but that's different from guilt. Or, as Tim Keller and I assert, they are certainly dealing with idols—the false worship of people, ideas, and things—and I think our application of God's message has to shift to deal with shame and idolatry.

Having said that, I do agree with N. T. Wright's definition of righteousness—that it carries associations with a life of justice. But I do worry that an over-balance from the idea of justification as "gift" to justification as "demand," because if we simply translate *righteousness* as "justice of God," then is not exactly good news for us, because we all patently fall well short of God's demands! It becomes another thing that is required from us, and it calls forth another form of the works-based righteousness that Paul and Luther were keen for us to avoid at all costs! Right relationship with God is not something that is within our power, and we can't produce this goodness enough to please God's demands. Actually, if righteousness is simply demand, then I think that's actually bad news and not good—because we are never going to be able to be right with God. We need to still see justification as the gift of God, but the gift demands a response of consistency.

CHRIS: It has to be God's justice that's restoring. God has to stay at the center because the temptation for all of us right now is to tell people that the Scriptures call *us* to care for the poor. And the kingdom of God is evident in these ways, but we have both been in communities with people who are seeking a kingdom, but without a King. You guys talk a lot about this in the book *ReJesus*, and you just go, "Man, this party is empty and the Groom hasn't shown up, and it doesn't feel like the kingdom anymore." So, again, this is a slippery slope that can lead to heresy, but if we keep our definition of *righteousness* as "God's restorative justice that we get to join in with," then God is the one making all things right. It is clearly not a work of our own.

ALAN: So if we've been justified, therefore we live lives that are consistent with that; therefore we are righteous in status if we live righteous lives. It very much comes back to Paul's indicative in the imperative: "You are this; now live your lives consistent with this." God restores us so that we might become agents of restoration.

DAN: I didn't even study the word *righteousness*, sadly enough, until we started Vintage Faith and we went through the

Sermon on the Mount. Actually, I am reading something from N. T. Wright's Web page right now that talks about what you just said. There are two scopes of meaning about it. It's developed from the Old Testament, and it basically says there are two fields of thought. One is righteousness defined as the right standing of a person in relation to a court's decision, and that's kind of how I have always viewed it. The other definition is "justice." I didn't even think of the justice part of it until six years ago; that was the first time.

CHRIS: When you began to teach through it, how did that transform you, and how did the teachings affect the church?

DAN: Well, I would say the Sermon on the Mount transformed the church, because that's where we chose to start the Vintage Faith Church teaching. Basically we said, let's start this church by walking through this passage. So all of the teachings of Jesus were shaping us from the beginning about who we wanted to be as a church. Santa Cruz Bible was a mega church; it was super contemporary, a very felt need, with a Bible-teaching Dallas seminary pastor. It wasn't a bad church at all, but they definitely focused more on our day-to-day actions in life: *Are we pleasing God with what we are doing or not?* So when you did think of righteousness, you were thinking more of your actions, your sin actions, and managing those. *Am I living a righteous life?* It's sort of the default thinking, and even how I taught about it.

CHRIS: And then when you went through the Sermon of the Mount . . .

DAN: We would sing, "Seek ye first the kingdom of God," but we never stopped to really think, *What does that really mean?* When you look at in the context of the entire Sermon on the Mount, it shapes everything, This wasn't just an isolated verse about sin issues and pleasing God. It became holistic in the "Are we living out the gospel?" discussion, whether it was about justice, or cheating your neighbor. The encompassing messages of the Sermon on the Mount are awesome. I think that was probably my biggest shift—seeing that righteousness is much larger than I ever thought.

CHRIS: It is puzzling to think how easily we miss all of this.

MARK: Yeah. I think *justice* is more of an active verb, while *righteousness* seems more static in today's language. It's a static word, and justice is often attached with the word *seek*—"seek justice," because it's something that *you* have to do. I think that the action orientation of that translation is a big deal, and, boy, isn't it interesting that the way that we translate these words can open up a whole different dimension of understanding? When I think about social justice issues (which have such resonance with our culture and with emerging generations), it does put things in a different light.

EIGHT

Shalom, the Fruit of Justice

Unfailing love and truth have met on their way; righteousness and peace have kissed one another.

— Psalm 85:10

Jesus had great hope for the prostitute, the thug tax collector, the adulterer, the leper, and the thief suffering the penalty of death. If any of these social outcasts were to inquire about redemption, he did not flinch. Forgiveness was standing before them. When someone in the self-righteous religious establishment approached him, such as Nicodemus or the rich young ruler, he did not quickly promise them Paradise, as he did the thief on the cross. Instead, Jesus asked the religious to sell all they had and give to the poor, or to be reborn. He seemed to be asking for the impossible from Nicodemus, but to the woman caught in adultery he offered forgiveness and simply asked her to sin no more.

The outcasts and degenerates, the people we would warn our children to avoid as the "bad people," seemed to be closer to the kingdom than the upstanding and seemingly righteous. How have we drifted so far from the heart of Jesus when it comes to broken people? Have we missed out on the kingdom by avoiding the people we are called to embrace? Jesus spoke in mysterious parables at times, but when it came to his love for the broken-down sinner and his insistence that we are in no position to stand as judge, he could not have been more clear.

If you judge *other people*, then you will find that you, too, are being judged. Indeed, you will be judged by the very standards to which you hold other people. Why is it that you see the dust in your brother's or sister's eye, but you can't see what is in your own eye? Don't ignore the wooden plank in your eye, but criticize the speck of sawdust in your brother's eyelashes. That type of criticism and judgment is a sham! Remove the plank from your own eye, and then perhaps you will be able to see clearly how to help your brother flush out his sawdust. (Matt. 7:1–5)

The Bible is clear that we are all sinners, but we want to put everyone in a category. Sadly, we have chosen to put people in boxes that are not helpful, but are incorrect and contrary to the truth of Scripture. Despite all of its merit, the Greek worldview has created a treacherous ground for Christianity. What the Hebrew viewed holistically, the Greek divided and dichotomized. Modern Christians have taken a previously integrated world and subdivided it into the sacred or secular, physical or spiritual, good or bad, profane or religious— categories that do not serve us well because they are simply untrue. God created the physical, and that makes it uniquely spiritual. The so-called "bad people" are also created in the image of God.

Growing up, we didn't have a lot of money, so we used to get outfield deck seats (aka "the cheap seats") to see the baseball games at the Astrodome. Most of the people buying the cheap seats did so to save more money for beer. After the first few innings, they were drunk, and by the time the seventh-inning stretch rolled around, there would be beer mixed with peanut shells on the floor, spilled beer down your back, and a brawl two rows over and back to the left. It was ugly out there. As a kid, I learned from a lot of people that we were sitting with the "bad people." (Could there be a more unchristian, or unbiblical, statement?) By the time we noticed someone drinking his second beer, we'd start pulling away from him.

There was this one consistent drunk fan named Batty Bob. He was a self-proclaimed Houston Astros mascot. He'd come to all the games wearing a rainbow wig, and he'd lead slurred cheers in the stands. I remember one time my dad went out to sit and talk with Batty Bob. He spent the whole game with Bob, then walked him out to the parking lot to bring him home with us. I was more than confused, because this guy was one of the "bad people." When we got home, my dad came to me and explained how God loved Batty Bob. I remember thinking, *Really? Batty Bob?* And he stayed with us for a few days to get back on his feet. This is when I started to realize that God did not despise these people; he dearly loved them.

Jesus became increasingly popular among *notorious* sinners—tax collectors and other social outcasts. The Pharisees and religious scholars noticed this.

Pharisees and Religious Scholars: This man welcomes immoral people and enjoys their company over a meal!

Jesus (*with another parable*): Wouldn't every single one of you, if you have 100 sheep and lose one, leave the 99 in their grazing lands and go out searching for the lost sheep until you find it? When you find the lost sheep, wouldn't you hoist it up on your shoulders, feeling wonderful? And when you go home, wouldn't you call together your friends and neighbors? Wouldn't you say, "Come over and celebrate with me, because I've found my lost sheep"? This is how it is in heaven. They're happier over one sinner who changes his way of life than they are over 99 good and just people who don't need to change their ways of life. (Luke 15:1–7)

Many Christians see the world this way, and are blind in their point of view. It's time to stop categorizing one another and call this line of sight what it is: heresy, specifically Gnosticism. Our broken ideology can be rescued when we forsake the "sacred versus secular" labels and see what has been redeemed and what is in need of redemption. People are not good or bad; they are simply broken, and God has either restored them to shalom or is seeking to restore them to shalom. Imagine seeing people as "broken shalom" or "shalom," rather than good or bad. If you see them in the midst of broken shalom, it does not allow you to look down on them; instead, it calls you to join God in his redemptive work in their lives. What a beautiful privilege.

I am passionate about the spiritual development of children, and I long to see churches get beyond the existing models of Christian education. We need to do much more than educate; we must disciple our children and set them within the mold so that as they grow, they can expand into an image of Jesus. It would be easy (in fact, it happens in churches today) to let kids who naturally see the world in black and white (Mommy is good; burglars are bad) to continue to put themselves (their presence, thoughts, and actions) and other people (and their presence, thoughts, and actions) into categories. But as we all learn through adolescence and adulthood, not much in the world is black and white. Every parent of older children knows this struggle. You have children who, for the first seven or so years, see nothing but the absolute best in you, no matter what you do. Even if they are really mad at you, you are never wrong. Then, as they move into their eighth, ninth, or tenth grade years, they start to realize that sometimes Mom and Dad aren't right. Sometimes Mom and Dad don't have all the answers, and in fact sometimes their solutions are wrong. Is Mom really bad? Is Dad not always right? It's painful on both sides. Parents become fallen gods; children become jaded.

We need to trust that God will meet us in the gray areas—in the places where burglars are transformed by grace and mommies make mistakes sometimes but hopefully make amends—to be willing to rip off the lens of "this is good, that is bad" and turn our faces to Jesus in these places where he will heal our faith. It is part of the great mystery. The prepackaged categories the church offers do not fit the real world. How can we expect our children to act in love and not fear if we are not portraying grace and redemption when we encounter or exemplify broken people, or when angry, abusive, and belligerent people unwittingly crash our lives? It will happen. We will encounter the argumentative drunk at the ballpark or the cursing parent in the grocery store. Telling our children that these people are bad does not offer them a biblical understanding; it is untrue. We have the chance to explain that shalom was broken in Eden, that Jesus restored shalom within our hearts with his sacrificial love, and that God can bring wholeness again to this broken world. Christine Sine explains the Hebrew understanding of brokenness:

Essentially the Fall unleashed the forces of "anti-shalom" ripping apart the harmony and mutual love of God's original creation. It broke God's shalom relationships and fractured the spirit of togetherness that bound us to God, to each other and to God's creation.

Exploitation, oppression, poverty, death and disease, war and violence, discrimination between male and female and across racial boundaries and the destruction and abuse of creation all gradually invaded our world as a result of the Fall.[1]

If we are raising young Christians to see things as good or bad, if we are making disciples who categorize things as sacred or secular, then we will be inclined to avoid the secular and vilify the bad; this is not the gospel according to Jesus. Could there be any pattern that seems less like the activity of Jesus? Our King did not enter into this fallen world to be a bystander amid brokenness. Just the opposite: he was drawn to it. As you read the Gospels, you would think Jesus aimed his path with GPS precision to the places where brokenness, disease, sickness, and depravity abounded most:

In Jerusalem they came upon a pool by the sheep gate surrounded by five covered porches. In Hebrew, this place is called Bethesda.

Crowds of people lined the area, lying around the porches. *As they walked among the crowds it became clear that* all of these people were *disabled in some way;* some were blind, lame, paralyzed, or plagued by diseases [and they were waiting for the waters to move. From time to time, a heavenly messenger would come to stir the water in the pool. Whoever reached the water first and got in after it was agitated would be healed of his or her disease.][2] In the crowd, Jesus noticed one particular man who had been living with his disability for 38 years. He knew this man had been waiting here a long time.

Jesus (*to the disabled man*): Are you *here in this place* hoping to be healed?

Disabled Man: Kind sir, I wait, *like all of these people,* for the waters to stir, *but I cannot walk. If I am to be healed in the waters,* someone must carry me into the pool. *So, the answer to Your question is yes—but I cannot be healed here unless someone will help me.* Without a helping hand, someone else beats me to the waters each time it is stirred.

Jesus: Stand up, carry your mat, and walk.

At the moment Jesus uttered these words a healing energy coursed through the man and returned life to his limbs—he stood and walked *for the first time in 38 years.* But this was the Sabbath Day, *and any work, including carrying a mat, was prohibited on this day.* (John 5:2–9)

In a cesspool of sickness and disease that all people would rightly avoid, Jesus walks right in and touches the suffering. He comes to us in the tradition of the Hebrew prophets, declaring the need for justice, but he enters the world in an entirely new way. He was not just calling God's people to change; he was making that change possible. Too often when we hear the word *prophet* we think of someone who has—or claims to have—supernatural powers. Prophets, we might think, are people who can predict the future, or who have a special connection to the Almighty, that the rest of us should listen to because they are taking cosmic dictation. But Jesus and the Jews of his day understood prophets in a different way. To them the prophets were the people given to the Jewish nation by God to tell them the hard truths, to call them to live in ways that honored God and not the false gods of power, wealth, sex, and security. They would, as Walter Brueggemann says, simultaneously paint us a picture of the world as it is and as it should be.

In the gospel of Luke, when Jesus announces what it is he has come to do, he announces it in the synagogue (where Jews had gathered to learn about the Scriptures) by reading a passage from the prophet Isaiah.

He eventually came to His hometown, Nazareth, and did there what He had done elsewhere *in Galilee*—entered the synagogue and stood up to read *from the Hebrew Scriptures.*

The *synagogue attendant* gave Him the scroll of the prophet Isaiah, and Jesus unrolled it to the place where Isaiah had written these words:

The Spirit of the Lord the Eternal One is on Me.

Why? Because the Eternal designated Me to be His representative to the poor, to preach good news to them.

He sent Me to tell those who are held captive that they can now be set free, and to tell the blind that they can now see.

He sent Me to liberate those held down by oppression.

In short, the Spirit is upon Me to proclaim that now is the time;

This is the jubilee season of the Eternal One's grace.[3]

Jesus rolled up the scroll and returned it to the synagogue attendant. Then He sat down, *as a teacher would do,* and all in the synagogue focused their attention on Jesus, *waiting for Him to speak.* He told them that these words from the Hebrew Scriptures were being fulfilled then and there, in their hearing. *His purpose was to fulfill what Isaiah had described.* (Luke 4:16–21)

What Jesus was saying was that the good news he had come to bring—the teaching and the healing that he was doing—had its basis in God's ongoing messages of justice and faithfulness. And that righteousness was not just about tallying our rights and wrongs; it was about a way of life in which people were called to justice and mercy and holiness all at the same time. The prophet Amos called his people to task and told them that if they continued to follow their culture's false gods instead of the God of Israel, it would be disastrous for them. What God wanted was not simply right worship and belief from His people, but for them to live lives shaped by justice and mercy.

Eternal One: I hate—I totally reject—your religious ceremonies.

    You think I delight in your solemn gatherings? I do not!

You can offer Me *whole* burnt offerings and grain offerings,

    but I will not accept them.

You can sacrifice your finest, fattest young animals as a peace offering,

    but I will not even look up.

And stop making that music for Me—it's just noise.

    I will not listen to the melodies you play on the harp.

Here's what I want: Let justice thunder down like a waterfall;

    let righteousness flow like a mighty river that never runs dry.

    (Amos 5:21–24)

What Amos and other prophets are telling us is that even before Jesus came to bring us God's good news, God was letting us know his desires. Abraham Heschel explains the prophets in vivid certainty:

Instead of dealing with the timeless issues of being and becoming, of matter and form, of definitions and demonstrations, [the reader of the prophets] is thrown into orations about widows and orphans, about the corruption of judges and affairs of the marketplace. Instead of showing us a way through the elegant mansions of the mind, the prophets take us to the slums. The world is a proud place, full of beauty, but the prophets are scandalized, and rave as if the whole world were a slum . . . To us a single act of injustice—cheating in business, exploitation of the poor—is slight; to the prophets, a disaster. To us injustice is injurious to the welfare of the people; to the prophets it is a deathblow to existence; to us, an episode; to them, a catastrophe, a threat to the world.[4]

These prophets also show us that people were either misunderstanding or ignoring what righteousness meant long before we were.

Isaiah, Amos, and Jeremiah all talk about those who think they know what God wants—right worship—but have ignored God's stronger command to be righteous. In his famous temple sermon, Jeremiah said, in ways that should convict many of us, that God's call to righteousness meant so much more than showing up for church.

> This is the message the Eternal One gave to Jeremiah. *A message delivered just as He instructed.*
>
> Eternal One: *Go now and* take a stand for Me at the entrance to My temple. Tell all of Judah to hear the Eternal One's words as they pass through these gates. *If they are supposedly* on their way to worship Me, *tell them to listen to Me, Jeremiah.* Tell them this is what I, the Eternal One, Commander of *heavenly* armies and God of Israel, decree:
>
> "Change your ways and *stop what you are* doing, and I will let you live in this land. Do not rely on the misguiding words *of the phrase,* 'The temple of the Eternal, the temple of the Eternal, the temple of the Eternal,' *as if the temple's presence alone will protect you.* But if you genuinely change your ways and *stop what you are* doing; if you deal with each other fairly; if you don't oppress the immigrants, orphans, and widows; if you don't shed the blood of the innocent in this place; *and if you* don't practice this self-destructive worship of other gods, then I will let you live in this land I promised to your ancestors forever and ever." (Jer. 7:1–7)

These were the scriptures that Jesus and the Jews knew, the wisdom from God that Jesus said in the Gospels that he had come to fulfill. The life of righteousness that we are supposed to live has been laid out for millennia, we just have been too blind or too weak or too stubborn to seize it. Righteousness is living out life through a restored, liberated heart made possible through Jesus. My friend

Greg Garrett points out in his book *Holy Superheroes* that we tend to understand *justice* (a familiar and misunderstood word for those of us in the American church) with connotations about right behavior and punishment of wrong behavior:

> Justice is more than punishment, a response to a negative action; it is also righteousness, a response to negative conditions. To think of justice simply as retribution and punishment for crimes committed is too limiting; just as the Anglican Book of Common Prayer's confession includes sins of commission, it also includes those things that we ought to have done, but didn't.[5]

In the Hebrew language, the word *tzedek* is often translated in the Bible as *justice*, but it has a much larger meaning—it can also be translated as *righteousness* or as *charity*. Justice—righteousness—is about putting yourself and the societal values to one side and trying hard to live in the God values that the prophets and Jesus have revealed about the healing of the world. When we think we are conforming to the letter of the law, when we believe we are putting God first by tithing or by attending church, we are really only grasping the very tiniest bit of what it is God wants from us. God wants us to be righteous— which means God wants us to be holy, healing, gathering, defending, and rescuing. God is all these things, just as Jesus did all these things. One more look at the Hebrew prophets can show us the movement from legalistic faith to a world-transforming faith. (Although we could do lots more study, I hope by now you're beginning to see how Jesus' Bible, the scriptures that shaped him, offer us valuable lessons.)

Two Hebrew words will shape our thinking about this last bit of Scripture. One is *tikkun*, a word that tells of the healing of the world; the other is *shalom*, a word sometimes used as a greeting or parting that means "peace," although its depth is greater than peace. It is more a picture of wholeness. It means "beauty." Shalom is a word that describes what the world will someday be, God willing. And *tikkun* is the word for our willingness to be part of it, for how our attempt to be righteous can lead to the beauty and love and healing God intends for all of us.

Isaiah says some prophetic things that should be familiar to us now. Isaiah calls to task the rich and the powerful and imagines a coming day when the needs of the needy will be filled, and the noble will act with nobility. Toward the end of this comes the promise of what will happen when people act with true righteousness:

> Then *the spirit of* fairness and truth will settle in the desert places,
>   and righteousness will infuse the fertile land.
> Then righteousness will yield peace, and the quiet and confidence
>   that attend righteousness will be present forever.
>   (Isa. 32:16–17)

As a Hebrew psalmist sang,

> Unfailing love and truth have met *on their way;/* righteousness and peace have kissed one another. (Ps. 85:10)

> Your rule is rooted deeply in justice and righteousness—/unfailing love and truth lead from the way ahead of You. (Ps. 89:14)

> The seed that flowers into righteousness will always be planted in peace by those who embrace peace. (James 3:18)

The broken can be restored by the love and grace of Christ, expressed through his people. What are the excuses holding you back from the beautiful adventure that is true Christianity? Like Jeremiah, is it your age? Have you become comfortable in religious circles and afraid to walk into the cesspools of your city? Gather some fellow disciples and walk with great purpose into the trailer parks, homeless colonies, gay bars, and government housing projects that surround you. You will be moved to redemptive action as you see the people you once labeled as "bad" through the eyes of Jesus.

PRAYER

Dear God, may we live as people with liberated hearts. We admit, God, that we gain confidence in the things we can figure out, and we feel good about things we can fix. Because of this, we often mark situations, people, and random things in our life as "good" and "useful," or "bad" and "trash." We not only box in your greatness, your love, but we box in our own and that of others. This is wrong. May we be willing to have the same vulnerability of love that you have shown us through your Son, our Savior Jesus. As your people, let our actions show your transformative love in places where shalom is broken. May we live obediently but freely and release our judgments on others, that they would know to whom we belong. May we seek residence with you always. May we abide in your shalom.

Interview with Alan Hirsch

Alan comes to his faith in Christ as a Hebrew believer, and his perspective on holiness is a gift that has the potential to richly bless your faith journey.

CHRIS: Alan, as churches approach the Sermon on the Mount and Paul's teaching in Romans that brings up righteousness repeatedly, what is your counsel in terms of how we should approach our study of the Scriptures in order to let the Bible be our guide on this topic?

ALAN: Well, I am always for Jesus first, then Paul, as Paul is my guide to Jesus (because Jesus is my Lord and not Paul). I think Jesus' concept of righteousness (if I remember correctly from when I dug into this years ago) is much more consistent with the Old Testament view, or the Jewish view. It has a sense of a demand about it, but it definitely has a more ethical connotation consistent with the lordship or the kingship of God, and that you must respond to that. And then Paul comes along and interprets the Christ event and the transfer of righteousness, and I think we need to hear both interpretations. I'm all for recovery of a Jesus-centered faith. He's the archetypal model of what it means to be a righteous person. He is the most righteous; therefore if he becomes the center point of our faith, how can we go wrong if we become more like Jesus? We should see the model in Jesus, and he should be the focal point that I should emulate. I should follow after him, become like him. And we need to hear Paul's interpretation that righteousness is a gift from God to us. Then we can live consistently with that knowledge. Keep your eyes on Jesus and receive the gift of God, as Paul would say. That would be the advice I'd give.

CHRIS: Part of what we're seeking in a holistic life of faith is a balance, and, especially as a Hebrew brother in Christ, I'd love to hear your perspective, Alan, on the church calendar and ritual. I feel like one of the places where we miss this righteous life is in neglecting the keys to a holistic life that are found in both feasting and fasting. We tend to be a people that do neither. We don't feast well; we don't fast well. We just kind of exist, and we get some fast food and we kind of just keep moving though life. How might the kind of consistent feasting and fasting that we see in the Old Testament illuminate our path to follow Jesus?

ALAN: In terms of general worldviews, the Hebraic worldview, or the monotheistic worldview, is very integrative and allows us to see all things within God's creation as things that are possibilities for holiness. The way that some people would describe it is that there are two realities of the world: the holy and the not-yet holy. Our job is to make them holy by bringing our intentionality, holy intention, to the task that we are confronted with day to day. So I think whether it be feasting or fasting, these can be holy things, and if they are not done with an eye toward God, then they can be unholy things.

The other thing is learning to be righteous in feasting (that is, in pleasure) and enjoying the good things that God has given to us. Sometimes it means that we need to give a gentle reprimand to ourselves, and that is the fasting piece. I'm much more of a feasting kind of guy myself. I think our job is to actually unite our pleasures; that which has potential to take us away from God needs more redemption, needs more direction in life. The challenge is much more than learning how to feast—we must learn how to feast unto God. And I think maybe you're right, that richer and liturgical life might help us in this area—having regular times with your brothers and sisters and having good food and wine together and feasting up and doing it as an act of holiness, not something divorced from God but filled with God intent.

NINE

The Ten Commandments of a Shalom Life

There are two ways to live your life. One is as though nothing is a miracle. The other is as though everything is a miracle.

—Albert Einstein

If your primary goal in life is to be effective, then I highly recommend that you read *The 7 Habits of Highly Effective People* by Stephen R. Covey. It's a good book, practical in the best sense of the word. Ultimately, the greatest value of any book (this one included) is the possibility that it will change your life, and the world, for the better. We all want to be more effective at what we do. The question is, what are we *supposed* to be doing in this world? If you become more effective at gaining worldly success, amassing enormous wealth, and isolating yourself, no one will be the better for it. The truth is that the resurrection of Jesus initiates a journey intended to bring shalom to all of creation. That includes our broken hearts, our broken relationships, our broken cities, and those living in extreme poverty across the globe.

Prayer is always a precursor of shalom. As we begin to see the brokenness that surrounds us, we must take these things to God and ask him to bring healing and wholeness. As we pray, there is much that we can do to receive God's healing work of shalom in our lives. From my observations in my own community, I have found that when we embrace the following patterns in our lives—I am calling them the Ten Commandments of Shalom Living—it leads us out of brokenness and into a Christ-centered completeness. I offer these habits to you humbly. They did not come to me inscribed in stone, but I strongly believe that you will be changed if you incorporate these ten practices into your life.

Fasting

If you are anything like me, you very often get what you desire. If I wake up craving barbecue or good Tex-Mex, I often find a way to move my lunch meeting to the desired location, and I savor those flavors with great satisfaction. We routinely get what we want, and the worst part is that we have come to expect getting what we want. The simple and beautiful gifts from God—the clean air that we breathe, our health, the joy of little children, and yes, good ole barbecue—are no longer gifts; they are rights. It goes something like: "I did this work over here, so I deserve this payoff over here. *I'm entitled.*" Entitlement is an aggressive cancer to the spirit. It will destroy you. Fasting may seem to be an extreme action to many: "So I should go without television for a week? Or fast from food and drink only juices? Abstain from computer use, or give up caffeine?" It is never easy, but fasting is a good dose of medicine for the tumor of entitlement.

I remember when Hurricane Ike hit the Texas coast a few years ago, and people went without electricity for weeks or longer. All the comforts of home just weren't so comfortable in the dog days of Houston humidity and heat without the extravagance of air-conditioning. I suddenly realized exactly how much I take for granted—that I can lazily reach over and flick on a light or a fan, or tap a button that digitally communicates to a machine the exact temperature I want the air to be. How I can run downstairs and add ice to my drink when it's getting warm, take a soothing bath in warm water, or look up any obscure fact quickly on the Internet. Those weeks were hard, but if you asked five million Houstonians about enduring weeks without electricity, the stories you will hear are beautiful. Neighbors gathered together for the first time to cook together outdoors; families read books, played board games, and interacted in ways they do not when their televisions and computers are wildly buzzing away.

Gratefulness is one of the clearest signs of healthy spirituality. When one has been given what one does not deserve, the heart should expand with hope and love. The opposite is also true. Entitlement is a sure sign of an unhealthy spiritual life. For me, a very simple realization recently broke my will, pride, and eventually my heart. I became aware that I am grateful for the enjoyment that food and material possessions bring to me, which is often substantial. In fact, I often joke about praying after meals because once I have savored the flavors, then I know how grateful I truly am. Yet I cannot remember the last time I was truly grateful for the food I was eating, for the fact that God was devotedly sustaining my life with a gift from his hand. I don't pray the Lord's Prayer, asking God to bring my daily bread, with a sense of urgency or dependence. I have come to expect that I will always have my daily bread. What about you? It is possible that in my mostly comfortable, predominantly agreeable life, I never have been truly grateful.

So I set out on a journey to rediscover what the Bible says about food, to connect with the poor, and to become a different man. Or at least I wished to try to know, or try to grasp at knowing how to genuinely be a grateful man. For forty days, I set out to journey with the poor, eating what they eat each day, which is mostly rice and beans. It was not easy for me, to say the least, and I constantly craved my favorite foods, but it changed me and infiltrated me in some really powerful ways.

Given our immense level of wealth in America, fasting is a most important and arduous discipline. Abstaining from the things we desire, denying the things we expect or have forgotten to be thankful for helps us realize that the world is definitely not centered around us and comfort is certainly not of the utmost importance. We begin to do more than merely consider the plight of the poor; we begin to truly see the destitute others around us. It is absolutely not a discipline we should take lightly. It's not a diet fad or a spectacle to prove to others how spiritual we are; this is the worst reason. Also, we shouldn't fast as a penance to atone for our sins. Jesus' penance was enough. If you do not fast righteously, that is, if you go in with wrong motives, abstaining to prove your piety to others, it will set you back miles rather than move you forward; it will contaminate your heart, not purify it. In Jesus' day, the religious establishment loved to make a big show of their commitment to God as they fasted. Before undertaking this type of production, heed the directions of Jesus:

> And when you fast, do not look miserable as *the actors and* hypocrites do when they are fasting—*they walk around town putting on airs about their suffering and weakness, complaining about how hungry they are.* So everyone will know they are fasting, they don't wash or anoint themselves with oil, *pink their cheeks, or wear*

comfortable shoes. Those who show off their piety, they have already received their reward. When you fast, wash your face and beautify yourself with oil, so no one who looks at you will know about your discipline. Only your Father, who is unseen, will see your fast. And your Father, who sees in secret, will reward you. (Matt. 6:16–18)

Feasting

One scandal whispered in scorn by those religious-establishment partisans about Jesus was a condemning criticism about his disciples for not evidencing their fasting. Actually, Jesus' disciples were often seen doing just the opposite of what the religious establishment did. Rather than dramatically denying themselves food in proper pious practice, the disciples were openly witnessed feasting in delight and abundance. Not only did they do this, but all this with known sinners and the ever-hated tax collectors. In the gospel of Luke, the Pharisees bring these charges to Jesus' attention:

Pharisees: Explain to us why You and Your disciples are so commonly found partying like this, when our disciples—and even the disciples of John—are known for fasting rather than feasting, and for saying prayers rather than drinking *wine.*

Jesus: Imagine there's a wedding going on. Is that the time to tell the guests to ignore the bridegroom and fast? Sure, there's a time for fasting—when the bridegroom has been taken away. Look, nobody tears up a new garment to make a patch for an old garment. If he did, the new patch would shrink and rip the old, and the old garment would be worse off than before. And nobody takes freshly squeezed juice and puts it into old, stiff wineskins. If he did, the fresh wine would make the old skins burst open, and both the wine and the wineskins would be ruined. New demands new—new wine for new wineskins. (Luke 5:33–38)

How blessed were they that Jesus the Son, our Bridegroom, our master of ceremonies, had not left the party. As Christians, we fast for the return and feast for the sacrifice that still gives us so much to celebrate. Too often devout people who take Jesus' call to care for the poor only fast regularly and center their lives around the needs of the poor, focusing on suffering alone. But they forget that the need to be celebrating God's grace, his creation, and his goodness is equally important.

A few years ago I made a pilgrimage to Kolkata (formerly Calcutta), India, attempting to seek spiritual direction. It is an epicenter of poverty and was the home of Mother Teresa. It was in this nucleus that I hoped to find the answers to an impasse in my faith. The twentieth-century heroine of the poor must certainly be the example of how I should live my life. Yet as I stood in the diminutive bedroom where Mother Teresa slept for more than fifty years, praying and reading the Scriptures, I heard an answer that I never expected. God did not tell me to give up all my possessions for the poor. He said, as clearly as I have ever heard him speak, "As equally as you care for the poor, *feast well!*"

While I was there, I had been reading a book that contained many private letters written by Mother Teresa. It offered a different side of this beloved saint than many might expect, and I learned from her own struggle and doubt in as many ways as I learned from her love and faithful service. In that book, she says to her spiritual director Michael van der Peet: "Jesus has a very special love for you. As for me, the silence and the emptiness is so great that I look and do not see, listen and do not hear."[1]

Teresa gave all that she had for the poor because so many in the

Western world were not willing to give anything. But along the way she seemed to lose the joy of her salvation. In fact, she says she went entire decades without feeling the love of Christ. It hurt me deeply as I read those words. With the greatest respect for Mother Teresa, I wish that she had taken more time with the Sisters of Mercy to feast together and celebrate the blessings of God as well as to identify with the suffering of Christ.

You may not be guilty of fasting too often, but if you are like most people in our culture, you neither feast nor fast; you merely exist. You eat enough processed food to keep your body moving. I've heard these rumors—legends mostly. Some say they're true; some say they're just stories. I can't be sure about what I am about to tell you, but in the "old days," long gone if they ever existed, people used to gather around this square object often made of wood . . . I think they called it a, taleb, no, a . . . table. They'd pull up chairs, similar to ours, just not in front of a TV or computer, and sit and talk to one another while they ate food. Actually talk and share food! Can you imagine? What a novel idea. There is nothing more sacred than worshipping God by spending time with family and friends.

I remember times growing up when my siblings and I would think throughout the day about something funny to say at dinner. My brother Brian was the best at it. We knew he was always going to bring something good. We'd laugh and tell of our highlights and hard times during the day. It brought us together. Feasting was also important for God's chosen people. The Hebrews saw it as a way to highly honor God. What did Abraham do when Isaac was weaned from his mother's breast? He hosted a feast to thank the Lord. It seems that anytime God did something amazing, they threw a big feast. Remember the prodigal son?

How often do you feast? Do you find you eat on the run often, or alone in your car, or at your desk? Is this typical for you? What does it look like to stop and eat with the people you love or are learning to love? Sharing the good days, sharing the bad days? How often do you especially savor the work of God's hands? This is the path of faith.

Living in Community and Seeking Brokenness Together

Do your problems often overwhelm you? Whether it's addictions, compulsive behavior, mounting debt, or a dead-end career, talking to others can greatly diffuse much of the stress. Brokenness and struggle are not nearly as intimidating when it is a shared experience. Whether it is your finances or the water crisis in Liberia, anything can be overcome when it is attacked together.

Back in 2000, in the early days of Ecclesia Houston, when my family consisted of my beautiful wife, Lisa; my daughter, Hanna; and myself, we encountered one of the greatest trials in our lives. After a night out with a friend, I went to rent a movie in order to enjoy some much-desired downtime. At the video store, my phone (the old Nextel two-way-radio sort) began screaming at me that my apartment was on fire. When I arrived at the house, I saw my startled wife and crying baby outside, and I instantly planned my defense. I would immediately run to get the extinguisher and start putting out the flames. I would take a deep breath, run in, spray the fire just as I had seen on TV hundreds of times, get back, and then repeat as required. I emptied several extinguishers that people were bringing to me as fast as I could grab them. It may have been minutes or an eternity when the fire department and paramedics arrived. I was graciously relieved of my heroic expectations and they insisted on giving me oxygen (I was fine).

The entire apartment was either torched or damaged by smoke

and water. In a flash we were homeless. Oh, and did I mention that Lisa found out that very night that we were pregnant with baby number two? In another wonderful streak of luck, my wife spent the next seven months of her pregnancy in extreme nausea, frequently bowing to a friend's toilet as we slept on their floor. It was stressful. Ugly. Painful. I'll never forget lying in bed that night, drenched in the smell of smoke, totally overwhelmed at being a father to a homeless family of four. The next day our community gathered for our quarterly love feast, and we had many offers to help with our laundry and cleaning, and we were given donations for cleaning supplies and meals. Over the course of the following week, we had several offers of places to stay, words of encouragement and prayer, and many people calling just to try and make us laugh. It was Jesus in action. The load was no longer too heavy to bear.

It's amazing how God's hands work. I want to call it a safety net, but it's more than that. It's the reality that we miss out on too often because we're impossibly busy trying to keep our own lives afloat. When tragedies and difficulties like Hurricane Ike or apartment fires come along and upturn our distorted, limited human reality, we must fall quickly into the hands of God, which are always there. It's my job to introduce people to a communal faith in Christ that says we are not alone in this world, that there is absolutely a God, and that together we voyage on our journey of faith, not as individuals but as a community, knitted together to catch each other as we fall. To safely cushion and protect each other from all the variety of causes and hardships that causes us to stumble, trip, or free-fall. Fellowship keeps us from hitting the bottom of those canyons flat on our faces and being utterly destroyed. It is sublime work. To be on the reciprocal end of this love is the most amazing gift next to Christ's grace and redemption.

Put Hands and Feet in the Dirt

When we spend time in nature, we become better people. The world of fluorescent lights, plastic chairs, polyester fabrics, and plastic-wrapped food is not the world we were made to inhabit. If you will take some time to put your hands in the dirt, your feet in the sand, and your eyes on a sunset, the way you view the world will begin to change: your grip on material things will begin to loosen, unforced conversations will flow, and prayer will happen as naturally as breathing.

Go to a place of beauty with people who love God and love you—camp, go to the beach, take a walk along the shore. Be reminded of the Garden. Understand that there is a created world that God set in motion, and that you are part of a running story, a poem in writing, a canvas before the artist, a harmonizing song. How often do you spend time in nature? Have you ever left a weekend of camping or a long walk in the woods and wondered why you don't do it more often? Listen to that voice. Reading Scripture is one way to learn about the heart of our God; spending time in his beauty is another. As his theme of death and rebirth plays out within your heart, pay close attention to the world that surrounds you—the crunch of dried fallen leaves, the crisp apple at harvesttime, the intense scent of evergreen, and the speckled flowers after the last drench of spring. Make time to be with God outdoors.

The psalmist calls us out to meet God in his creation:

The earth and all that's upon it belongs to the Eternal One.
     The world is His, with every living creature on it.
With seas as foundations and rivers as boundaries,
     He shaped the continents, fashioned the earth.
Who can *possibly* ascend the mountain of the Eternal One?

Who can stand before Him in sacred spaces?
Only those whose hands have been washed and hearts made pure,
 men and women who are not given to lies or deception.
The Eternal One will stand close to them with blessing *and mercy
 at hand,*
and the God who redeems will right what has been wrong.
 (Psalm 24:1–5)

The psalmist understood what our hurried lives often ignore: the movement of creation is gracefully stirring toward shalom. When we step into that current and follow that flow, we find that God is near and has never been far removed, despite the pervasive load of life's struggles.

Live Reconciled to One Another (Whenever Possible)

It is easy for us to allow friendships to fall by the wayside when they require a bit of work. Even the word *friend* has become so commonplace that it may have lost its meaning. I have five thousand "friends" on Facebook; some I have never met, and others will quickly remove me as a friend if I post something that they do not like. Is that friendship? I don't think so. I am sure King Solomon, who taught the wisdom of true friendship in Proverbs, would find our modern definitions laughable. We all crave the security that comes with having a handful of true friends, the kind of people that Solomon describes in Proverbs 17:17: when trouble comes your way, many will desert you, but a true friend steps forward declaring, "I was born for this day, to stand with you in adversity." If you have even one friend like this, you are wealthy beyond measure.

You don't make true friends by accident. As Winnie the Pooh says, "You can't stay in your corner of the forest waiting for others to come to you. You have to go to them sometimes." Pursuing true friends may be a lost art. We need to learn how to seek out people of character, cultivate a commitment to them, and teach our children to do the same. Friendships are tested in times of conflict; they are strengthened when we walk through hard times together, when we learn to forgive. As we come to realize that we have a friendship deficit, there is rarely someone else to blame; the cause is almost always that we have not been a good friend to others.

One of the best attributes a friend can have? Proximity: "Do not neglect your friend, or your parent's friend, *for that matter*. When hard times come, you don't have to travel *far* to *get help from* family; A neighbor who is near is better than a brother who is far away." (Prov. 27:10). The wisdom of King Solomon is still true today; the best friends are close friends, as in friends who are able to come to you when your car won't start, or help you carry out your old mattress, or, unlike Job's friends, friends who know when to shut up and just sit there with you. Honestly, the kind of friends that can sit with you quietly on a long drive or share a simple meal with a few kind words may be the best friends of all. The enemies of true friendship have been whitewashed in our day; gossip is now chitchat, usury is networking, and betrayal is an accepted custom of daily life. May we seek to emulate the character of people like E. M. Forster, who once said, "If I had to choose between betraying my country and betraying my friend, I hope I should have the guts to betray my country." Amen.

Be Real

Visions of the church often spring up in the strangest places. I spent a year in high school working evenings and weekends for a small company that recorded Alcoholics Anonymous meetings and sold the tapes to alcoholics who were longing for constant encouragement in their struggle to stay sober. As I have said before about my teenage years, it was a point in my personal journey of faith when I had become pretty disillusioned with what I saw in the church. Our Sunday gatherings were the place where we had to get all cleaned and fixed up to portray that proper so-called Christian image, sing the great hymns, read Scripture, and come together with all of God's people—who happened to agree with the dress code and doctrine and believed what they chose to from the Bible. The makeup and perfume were masking more than foul odors or the emerging acne of my teenage peers. Not only did people look their best; they also looked their wealthiest. Church back then seemed to be more about hiding the truth of what we were—hiding our nakedness—than it was about Christ. Sin was what other people did, and the really bad sins were the ones that we believed we and those we loved would never struggle with. So we put our best face forward, bragged about our good deeds, and hid all the rest.

So you can imagine that while I was accepting that world as truth, I was totally surprised as I sat in that recording studio office, listening to meeting after meeting of people whose faith was mostly Christian, speak with an honesty that I had never heard before. They started by saying their names and confessing that they were powerless over alcohol. After this initial disclosure, they would circumspectly admit their sins and varying struggles: *I am gay . . . I am fat and I eat to relax . . . I masturbate habitually . . . I am a diabetic and I eat sugar all the time, despite the reality that it is killing me . . . I lose my temper and yell at my kids . . . I spend money that I don't have on alcohol and things I don't need . . . I live in fear of not being accepted . . . I use violence to intimidate the people I love the most . . . I pay people for sex . . . I killed my cousin in a drunken rage . . . I drink to cope . . . to forget . . . to ignore . . . to medicate . . . to find false courage . . . to feel loved.*

To put it lightly, these people were broken, and yet there was beauty in their catharsis that was life cleansing for both them and me. Through the process of being honest about their circumstances, they were pouring out poison that was destroying their lives and taking the first steps toward healing and getting better. It was amazing! I had never experienced anything like it before. Jesus was at work healing these people, sitting next to them, helping them identify their pains and transgressions, giving them the words to say, and holding them while they cried. From my earliest years in church, I had heard stories and testimonies of and from people who had premarital or adulterous sex, depended on drugs and alcohol, lied, cheated, and stole before they met Jesus and turned their lives away from sin, but I had never actually witnessed or encountered people in the midst of struggling with their demons and wrestling with their sin. More than a removed story or testimony, these confessions were the precise and vulnerable moments of admission to brothers and sisters, instances of receiving forgiveness and liberation from the cancerous bonds that were destroying them, and the offering of encouragement from a loving community providing the assistance with the first steps toward the acceptance of grace and redemption.

I even had a thought at the time (more than a fleeting fancy, but less than a convicting directive) that I should become an alcoholic so that I could know what community practiced in this way would actually feel like, but then I remembered a book in the Bible called Acts that vividly describes how, in the early days of the church, people shared everything; they shared more than just money and resources, but they shared of themselves—their encouragement, forgiveness, accountability, and most important, their love. They were people (not different from the ones in those meetings) willing to go down into the depths with one another; to share in the richness of life with one another. *That* is what I wanted!

How emancipating from the humdrum would it be if I could devote my life to shaping Christ's bride, the church, to become a place and body of safety, beauty, and hope? In other words, to become a place of shalom. This passionate reaction stayed with me, and years later, in my early years as a pastor, I learned a very important lesson that added even more to this awareness. It was in the mid 1990s when my friend David Crowder and I started University Baptist Church in Waco, Texas. As a twenty-three-year-old, I was still learning the ropes and finding my voice. Sundays were . . . tough. Services started very early and consisted of a challenging setup in the old downtown theater that our growing church rented. One particular Sunday I woke up late. While rushing to the shower, I stubbed my toe on the bed, which I am sure many of you know is among the most painful experiences known to man. This was more than a surface wound, friends. It was ugly and painful and it was only through a true miracle that I made it through the experience.

As I hobbled through my sermon, I explained the circumstances of the painful incident and confessed that I blurted out some of the foulest words I had ever learned. Suffice it to say, I did not anticipate the response that I received from that confession. Half the room seemed to pull away from me as if I had leprosy. I had offended them just by admitting my imperfection. They were scandalized that a pastor would be human and flawed enough to curse. Thankfully, the other half of the room seemed to draw closer to me. Instead of being displeased, they were actually relieved by my humanity. A realization washed over me, and the clarity of that moment resonated within me: I knew in the depths of my heart that I was called to live in community with people that were honest enough not to pretend that if they experienced sudden, unexpected pain, they would react by first reminding themselves of the terrible sin of cursing and then calmly sing hymns to dispel the agony.

In times of rest we often receive the greatest insights. I was recently blessed with the opportunity to go on a sailing trip to the British Virgin Islands with some friends from our church. During this voyage I was reminded of the important New Testament principles of a healthy community in ways I had never imagined. I only agreed to go on the trip because, of course, I love Jesus much more than most people, and I am willing to experience sin and redemption, pain and suffering, and because I want to fully understand Jesus, who coincidentally spent significant ministry time on sailboats. Who am I kidding? What an awesome, amazing chance of a lifetime! Anyway, despite the risk of sounding like a third-rate Bill Hybels, who creates metaphors of sailing with skill and beauty, I would like to tell you how a week sailing the treacherous waters of the Caribbean offered me amazing insights into life as a commissioned community of believers.

There were seven of us who signed on for this perilous adventure, all men from my home church, Ecclesia. Please allow me a momentary digression to discuss the meaning of the word *ecclesia*. It means "gathering," or "body of component members," essentially "church"—those called out to live (spiritual and physical) life together. Preparing for this trip, I was ill equipped to receive the understanding, recognition, and appreciation that I would have never guessed I would encounter, let alone spiritually process and acquire during this trip. I was simply prepared for fun in the sun and flip-floppin' good times. What I left with, what stuck with me besides the fun and memories, was the incredible, sublime beauty of community and redemption. One of the best ways to establish this transcendental awareness is by installing seven good-sized men into the galley of a cramped sailboat. This situation highlighted one of the greatest challenges we all face at one point or another—climbing out of ourselves so that we can authentically *live*. What I mean is that we must learn to openly *absorb* love, trust, generosity, and acceptance, right alongside one another.

One of the most insightful and accurate statements I have ever heard was spoken in parting words from my friend Paul's wife, Kristin. She said, "The outcome of this trip will be that these guys are going to either totally love each other or totally hate each other." At the time it simply struck me as a rather bizarre statement. I wasn't sure if she was just being negative. I thought we were just taking a vacation together and that we would naturally all have a great time and everything would be good. Impressively, she was absolutely right. The real beauty and worth of the journey would not be found in the landscapes we sailed, but it resided in our interactions with one another. It reminded me of what my brother and I dreamed and prayed over during the birth of Ecclesia:

How will we live together in and as a community?
How will we treat one another?
Will we get beyond ourselves and become a component of a
  machine designed to accomplish something much more
  significant in the world than mere self-edification?
What will that look like?
When we sail into a storm, will we capsize and die?

Thrown together on a boat, we had ourselves a situation to figure out: *How would we relate to one another?* Truly, how we relate to one another is unbelievably important. Fellowship among Christians should be designed in the same way. We are to be as travelers on a ship, all playing a role in riding through the storms and individual struggles together, with the unconditional love of Jesus our Captain.

I am thankful that, in my community, I rarely get a pat answer when I ask people how their lives are going. When times are tough, I just put a hand on their shoulder and pray for them as they go through life's challenges and hope that they will learn what they need to learn from those times and adversities. I know it is not always going to be easy, but I know earnest prayer and concern heals and accomplishes miracles.

Pursue Others Beyond the Surface

By doing this, you create trusting relationships that expose, and yet also protect, the heart. Take the time to seek one another genuinely. Each night on the boat, instead of playing poker as we had previously planned (because they all knew and were afraid I'd take them to the cleaners), it was suggested that we share our life stories with one another. Out there under the stars and resting on the waves, it just felt right. So each night, our group of men, with a span of wisdom that reached from the ages of early thirties to sixties, shared a meal, relaxed together, and listened as each of us shared his own story.

A magnificent love and respect grew for one another as each teller spoke of the broken parts of his life. We all told of the shattered and damaged sections of our hearts and minds in our stories. Some of us haven't completely come to grips with all of the displaced pieces of our hearts yet, but we're all on our way there, and sharing with one another was probably the most beneficial step we've taken yet.

I often receive phone calls the night before someone is about to open up his or her life story in a small-group setting, asking me if he really has to tell his *whole* story, or if he can give the PG version because, truthfully, I think we are deeply afraid that, *If they really knew me, if they really knew all of my story, there's no way they would love me*. Right? Every time, without exception, as people begin to share their stories, fear eats its way in. It happens in these groups and it happened on the boat. This cannot be allowed. Love conquers fear. Whenever the threat of fear asserted itself, the circle of men on that boat would literally hug and embrace as listeners created a protective wall around the teller in their time of brokenness. This is the same that should happen in all situations of confession, sharing, and testimony.

The truth is, most of us aren't bound together around our perfection, and perfect people don't exist. I've never met one, and as James says, the person who's mastered his tongue is perfect (3:2), and I don't know anyone who has mastered the art of stubbing their toe without completely and utterly losing momentary control of all faculties and blurting out at least *one* less-than-pious word. People do not truly meet one another in places of superficiality and portrayals of perfection. People meet in the crushed and fractured places. It is in our moments of weakness when the members of Christ's body are to crowd in, physically admitting and agreeing, "I am with you. I am broken like you are. I love you, and I am not going anywhere."

What does it mean to pursue others in relationship? When was the last time you were pursued beyond just the standard A + B = C conversation: "Hey, how are you doing?" "What do you do for a living?" Conversations like that aren't even a floating drift on the surface compared to being honestly pursued about your depths. "Who are you? I would like to know you." I desperately pray that in our community we can honestly say that even though we don't know everyone, we are seeking to truly know one another, to get beyond the surface, into a place of honesty and reality. In the act of pursuing one another, a space is created to be real, open, and honest. In this space we are *supposed* to be allowed to acknowledge our greatest failures, including those that have hurt others and the people we love the most, and believe that we will be redeemed.

If you are isolated, perhaps you need to be thrown into a boat with someone; to have to live in close proximity with others and have to figure out how to live in *togetherness*. I pray that when this happens, it happens for you as it did for us that week. I pray that you are able to be honest and real with those close to you, to pursue one another, and to assist in liberating one another.

Something else that is surprising for me, and one of the things many people learn in life, usually in corporate settings, is that power structures often rock the boat. On a boat, someone has to be in charge—someone who knows how to sail. And, just like in a business, how that hierarchy plays out dictates the success of the entire ride. If you have a captain who knows how to sail, but is a dictator, odds are you'll have a mutiny. On our voyage, our friend and captain shared his power in a brilliant way that was beautifully effective, even coronating his son-in-law as the captain on the second leg, despite the fact that he didn't have nearly as much sailing experience. When you live in a space where power is shared and not hoarded, glorious things begin to happen. At times, you're going to be the captain, and you're going to tell me to go and pull this rope or tie that rope, and I am going to do it. At other times the opposite will be true. We're called to respond and work as a team and not to wrestle for power or clench fists to hold on to control. We're going to choose to serve one another and play our part in this beautiful, redemptive narrative. We're going to steer this ship and keep it afloat despite the crashing of the waves and the blowing of the wind.

Recently my friend Greg Holder shared a sermon here at Ecclesia, and after the trip, the words he spoke struck me much more than they would have before. He spoke of lines. Wherever we are, we draw lines. But whatever lines are drawn, it's our job to erase them. It's our job to cross over these man-made distinctions and labels to bring people together. What helped sink this message into my ocean was a discovery we made of an interesting division in the categories of people who sail the high seas. There are the luxury sailors, who sit on their boats and sip cabernet while eating Gouda cheese; and there are the fishermen, who throw back Old Milwaukee while crunching pork rinds. Between these two classes exists a certain animosity. The sailors hate the fisherman because they cut across in front of their boats and steal their wind. We were new to this, so we weren't really sailors, and out of ignorance in regard to the divisions on the high seas, we brought along our fishing poles (not that we caught any fish, so I guess we're not fishermen either). Just try to picture us on our sailboat, towing our lines behind us, clearly misfits to both groups of people. The sailors didn't really like us because we were such amateurs, and the fishermen didn't claim us for more or less the same reason. But because we were on both sides and neither side of the line between the two groups, we were somewhat able to transfer between the two and strike up a conversation with either of them. We may have been despised, but we did our best to be all things to all people. We had learned that the truth of community is that there are no distinctions besides those we draw ourselves, and this lesson helped give us the confident knowledge that we could walk through any fences.

That's what the gospel is about. Beauty is invited in when we pursue one another and discover there's no Jew, there's no Gentile, there's just all of us. All of us are God's children. As Christians, we are called to exist in a place where people of totally different ethnic classes, cultures, races, creeds, and religious backgrounds come together as one community and say, "We want to walk alongside each other."

We desperately need to be part of communities where fences are being torn down, where we're drawn together with people who aren't like us, where we are willing to learn from one another, where beautiful things begin to happen.

Be Generous

It's easy to think that generosity begins when you have great wealth. We always seem to say, "I'll support such and such cause when I get a raise," or "I'll up my tithe when I get married," or "I'll adopt those children when I get that new job." But real giving doesn't happen when it's comfortable and easy; it just doesn't work out that way. The time for generosity is now. In the early days of the church, generosity was about sharing not what was convenient, but sharing everything:

> *During those days,* the entire community of believers was deeply united in heart and soul to such an extent that they stopped claiming private ownership of their possessions. Instead, they held everything in common. The apostles with great power gave their eyewitness reports of the resurrection of the Lord Jesus. Everyone was surrounded by an extraordinary grace. Not a single person in the community was in need because those who had been affluent sold their houses or lands and brought the proceeds to the emissaries [literally, *apostles*] of the Lord. They then distributed the funds to individuals according to their needs. (Acts 4:32–37)

Generosity is not about how much you have; it is about how you hold on to or let go of the material possessions that you have been given. Even if you have worked for it, and "earned" it, your path toward your current state was made possible by God, and anything that you may possess now is a gift. Would you have *earned* it if you had been born somewhere else, in other circumstances? The reality is that if you are tightfisted with your possessions now, you will hold on even more tightly when you possess more in your hands. At some point, money starts to possess you, and not the other way around. If you have little, learn to be generous with what you have. It is time to let go; our possessions are not a problem if we hold them loosely. They do not belong to us anyway. Our tight grip on those things is choking the joy out of life.

How would you describe your posture as it relates to material possessions? Are you fixated on gaining more? Do you label all your food in the office refrigerator as a warning to anyone who might sample your goods? How often do you loan out your car to a friend in need? What are you holding on to tightly? For some it is a car, for others an online video game world, for someone else it's clothes—today's vices are as varied and unique as today's individuals.

A specific couple, who are good friends of mine, decided to examine their relationship with possessions and take action to loosen their grip. I am sure we all can deeply relate to their struggle. Over the course of a couple of decades, my friend had repeatedly lost his temper with his wife when she inevitably backed into something, or someone, and knocked an unsightly dent or a bright shining scratch in an otherwise well-cared-for car. She was, shall we say, prone to small mishaps, and he would become flustered and angry about every incident. In these confrontations they would end up unreasonably angry at one another, and over what? A thing! A thing built from carbon matter that will eventually return to dust. They decided to seek a solution. Now it is their routine procedure that the day they bring home a new car, they first and foremost make a preemptive strike with a small ping hammer. This first dent sufficiently tarnishes the perfect finish and shape. Damage done. No reason to get fired up when the next dent comes along.

Loosening your grip is hard to do. Sometimes you need to take a hammer to whatever it is that is preventing you from being liberated. What is it that you hold on to too tightly? How can you take a hammer to it? It is *just* a thing, after all. Jesus did not avoid providing us with rather specific directions regarding how to create the proper attitude toward our stuff:

> Here is the bottom line: do not worry about your life. Don't worry about what you will eat or what you will drink. Don't worry about how you clothe your body. Living is about more than merely eating, and the body is about more than dressing up. Look at the birds in the sky. They do not store food for winter. *They don't plant gardens.* They do not sow or reap—and yet, they are always fed because your heavenly Father feeds them. And you are even more precious to Him than a beautiful bird. *If He looks after them, of course He will look after you.* (Matt. 6:25–26)

When we worry about acquiring even the most basic of human needs, Jesus says we show little faith. How much less should we worry about a 56-inch LCD TV? How much less should we worry about scratches on a status symbol that masquerades as a vehicle? Jesus also wanted each of us to understand our role in financing the kingdom and the work of the kingdom. In order to highlight this message, Jesus offered the following insight to his disciples by bringing true generosity in action to their attention:

> Jesus sat down opposite the treasury, where people came to bring their offerings, and He watched as they came and went. Many rich people threw in large sums of money, but a poor widow came and put in only two small coins[2] worth only a fraction of a cent.
>
> Jesus (*calling His disciples together*): Truly, this widow has given a greater gift than all the other contributions combined. All the others gave a little out of their great abundance, but this poor woman

has given God everything she has. (Mark 12:41–44)

The teachings of King Jesus wipe away all our excuses. A life marked by shalom will not come to us in our selfish and greedy states. Ask God to help you learn to share freely and to be free from all slavery to your possessions. It starts today.

See the World Through the Eyes of Jesus

It is time we really, truly, fully embrace beauty and laughter when it is before us. Most of us live at such a rapid pace that we rarely stop to listen to God's voice. When we were sailing, we'd regularly stop everything in order to witness the sun as it was sinking low in the sky and seeming to dip down into the water, the colors blowing up and then fading out—there was simply no other option than pausing and taking it in. We were encountering beauty face-to-face. If you'd only pause to look, you'd encounter the same beauty every day, wherever you are. When we take the chance to see what Jesus sees, and laugh a little along the way, the world is different. We need to learn to laugh more with and at one another and at ourselves.

We must understand that we see the world through very unique and limited lenses, and that they often do not align with a biblical worldview. We all assess every situation, political issue, or social ill through a lens we have formed throughout each of our lives that is cluttered with a host of individual experiences. These lenses project a light that is forever stained with the colors of our memories and upbringing. You might evaluate immigration reform from the perspective of a taxpayer, or see the neighborhood drug dealer from the perspective of a protective parent. Jesus would likely see these situations in a completely different light. In Houston I can travel a few blocks and see hundreds of immigrants standing on a street corner, asking for work. These men are not asking for my charity; they want to work in order to feed their families back home. As a U.S. citizen you might be infuriated by illegal immigration, and that seems reasonable, but as a Christian, you should realize that the Bible could not be more clear on the subject. Which citizenship do you take more seriously? Your country or the kingdom? The Scriptures tell us: "When an alien lives with you in your land, do not mistreat him. The alien living with you must be treated as one of your native-born. Love him as yourself, for you were aliens in Egypt. I am the LORD your God" (Lev. 19:33–34 NIV).

Try to imagine where Jesus would go in your city. How would he be moved? Really, how would Jesus respond to the people in need around us? Jesus' opinion on how to treat people—strangers, immigrants, or otherwise—isn't hidden on any lost scrolls:

King: . . . *You shall be richly rewarded,* for when I was hungry, you fed Me. And when I was thirsty, you gave Me something to drink. I was alone as a stranger, and you welcomed Me *into your homes and into your lives.* I was naked, and you gave Me clothes to wear; I was sick, and you tended to My needs; I was in prison, and you comforted Me.

Even then, the righteous *will not have achieved perfect understanding, and say that they don't recall visiting Him in prison or clothing Him.*

Righteous: Master, when did we find You hungry and give You food? When did we find You thirsty and slake Your thirst? When did we find You a stranger and welcome You in, or find You naked and clothe You? When did we find You sick *and nurse You to health?* When did we visit You when You were in prison?

King: I tell you this: whenever you saw a brother *or sister hungry or cold*, whatever you did to the least of these, so you did to Me. (Matt. 25:35–40)

We may suddenly find one day that we are the poor, imprisoned, or "the least of these." How might we understand this passage if our roles were reversed with a disabled homeless man? The truth is that our lives are not always sailing on smooth water. At any time we may be struggling to survive like the apostle Paul when he survived a shipwreck only by holding on to a small, floating piece of the ship. In the blink of an eye, a sudden catastrophe could befall us and we would find ourselves barely holding on, simply hoping and praying to survive. Our lifeline is supposed to be the church. We aren't just called to care for one another; we are commanded to. We must abandon our plans to simply create tremendous programs to help people and actually find some people to live with—up close and personal, caring for one another as Christ has cared for us.

Love God and Pursue Your Dreams

Saint Augustine said it best: "Love God and do what you will." Love God and he will put you on the path to pursue your dreams, whether you are currently aware they are your dreams or not. You are an emissary of King Jesus, which means he has given you the authority to act on his behalf. Your life, therefore, has *great* meaning. Jesus promised that his followers would do even greater things than he did. He is no liar, and I know he was not exaggerating. When you love God, he will gift you with big dreams. These won't be dreams for you alone, but for a transformed world.

Remember the story in the gospel of John about Jesus going to the pool of Bethesda and healing one of the men (John 5:2–18)?

It is only one story of the many acts of health care provided by Jesus. This pool was a known gathering place for the sickest of the sick. If Jesus healed one man by the pool, what does it look like for us to be part of an even greater miracle? Could an entire village be healed? It is a guarantee that there are places of sickness and disease similar to this in your city. When was the last time you went and offered help? Have you ever spent much time in a county hospital? If you want to be used by God today, go to the cafeteria in your city's public hospital. Bring enough money to buy someone coffee and pray for them; be prepared to be changed by the experience. If you are not, mail me the receipt and I will gladly pay for the coffee.

In the so-called third world, there are entire villages plagued by malaria, AIDS, malnutrition, and countless preventable illnesses. We as Christians are capable of stepping into these places and seeing an entire village or more healed. Pregnant mothers are the most vulnerable and in need of help since they're already struggling to get enough nutrition to sustain one person, much less two. In countries like Haiti, it is a great challenge to see children survive even their first few years.

I am grateful for organizations like Compassion International, who offer each of us the opportunity to join Jesus at the pool of Bethesda as we serve pregnant women in impoverished countries and clothe and feed children. A church that raises $25,000 will fully fund a Child Survival Center, which will serve between forty and oe hundred mother-child groups for an entire year and change an entire village.[3] I think these are the things that Jesus was talking about—walking into a place where mothers often buy coffins for their babies before they are even born and giving care where there would be death—an entire village transformed. That is a miracle!

Miracles also take place in places you have likely been avoiding.

With the subtlest words of kindness, Jesus has the power to alter the state of lonely people. If we allow Jesus to speak through us, we, too, can reach out as he did when he was in a Samaritan village:

> In a *small* Samaritan town known as Sychar, Jesus *and His entourage* stopped to rest at the historic well that Jacob gave his son Joseph. It was about noon when Jesus found a spot to sit close to the well while the disciples ventured off to find provisions. *From His vantage, He watched as* a Samaritan woman approached to draw some water. *Unexpectedly* He spoke to her.
>
> Jesus: Would you *draw water and* give Me a drink?
>
> Woman: I cannot believe that You, a Jew, would associate with me, a Samaritan woman, much less ask me to give You a drink.
>
> Jews, you see, have no dealings with Samaritans. *Besides, a man would never approach a woman like this in public. Jesus was breaking accepted social barriers with this confrontation.* (John 4:5–9)

Loneliness is not picky. People are lonely in crowded rooms. They are sitting alone at bars and coffee shops, in chairs right next to yours. Don't blaze in with tracts and all *your* answers. I know it's tempting, but go in easy. Ask yourself the question, "How can I love well today?" If you go in with nothing else on the agenda than being a heart willing to befriend strangers, you will do well. I am certain that dropping by the local watering hole with a faithful friend once a week, you will find yourself in spiritual conversations that you couldn't have imagined (those are the best kind) as the Spirit of God begins to work on the people that you talk to. Some will come to faith in Jesus. Best-case scenario, it is the bartender. (I have learned that when a bartender or barista comes to faith, dozens often follow them.) Let's be honest—you need to be more like Jesus. You need to sit at the smoky bar (I know; I have allergies too) and learn to love drunk people. I am quite sure it is what Jesus would do.

In John 10:10 Jesus says "I came to give life with joy and abundance"; this is shalom living. Not one of us dreams as a child that we could grow up to become church attendees who drop a few dollars in the plate and live our own lives. We hope to be part of changing the world. As we lean into these rhythms of life, the beauty of true Christianity becomes our present reality rather than a distant dream.

PRAYER

God, we long to be in your presence. We are faulty—selfish and insecure. We are afraid and we often believe in nonsense. But now we come to you, ready to lay it all down to be a part of your movement to love and restore people. Take on our hearts, God; wrap them in your passion. Teach us to live communally as you live. Show us how to live well. Give us your vision of shalom; we beg for your compassion for people and places where shalom is broken. You are infinite; you are mighty; you are beyond all comprehension and expectation. Let our words be yours; let our actions show that your love endures. In Jesus' name, Amen.

Afterword

July, 2010

The journey of writing a book is transforming in almost every way. For months upon months you are immersed in a subject, and in this case the Scriptures. In a season of prayer, thought, and contemplation, I await the creative rush of articulating ideas and connecting others with life-changing truths. I have had the privilege many times of writing a book that contains a message that is important to me, one that I long for people to grasp and that I believe can transform their lives. This is the mission of a pastor, author, and ultimately of every believer in Jesus the Liberating King. But this book is so much at the core of a healthy understanding of the gospel, and so much the essence of my calling, that the experience has been amplified in every way.

At the completion of this book, I took several months to contemplate this simple afterword. I wanted to offer some words of encouragement, hope, and inspiration, as well as a plan of action—a way to see that the faith that has grown as we have journeyed through these chapters together could begin to bear fruit in our lives, our cities, and in the world. I struggled to complete this afterword until I made a trip to New Orleans, Louisiana, to visit with church leaders and national faith leaders, tour the oil-tainted oceans with local fisherman, and contemplate God's power to redeem this part of His creation.

In an earlier chapter I wrote about my general curiosity and my constant pursuit of conversations that lead us ultimately to a better understanding of the *imago dei* that resides in all of us. These conversations will lead back, if we allow them, to biblical truth that will always center ultimately in the person of Jesus Christ. I have enjoyed many conversations with people who work on offshore rigs, people who have designed offshore rigs, or those who design certain parts or elements or mechanical facets of these rigs. Life on a small platform on the open seas sounds like a challenge to me, and I am amazed that we are able to drill into very, very deep waters to do work that seems almost impossible. Yet, somehow, engineers and oil-field workers are able to execute these tasks in an ocean full of waves and turbulence. I had no idea that when I wrote those words that this curiosity would be cracked open in a brand-new way on the day the Horizon offshore rig, owned and operated by British Petroleum, exploded, killing eleven people and beginning a journey that will change not only the face of Louisiana, Alabama, Florida, and Texas, but the entire U. S. and possibly far beyond.

As I write these words, the oil continues to gush. It is not a spill. A spill is something radically different. This is a gusher that up to this moment has not been stopped. And, like many of you, as I watched the painful footage from the submersible camera that clearly shows the volume of oil and methane exploding from this broken pipe, I found that I can only stand to watch very small portions of this footage, and of the relief efforts and of the many oil-stained birds, dolphins, and sea turtles. It seemed that any more than fifteen minutes of CNN coverage would send me into a dark hole of depression. So I was reluctant and fearful when I accepted an invitation to join a group of faith leaders in New Orleans to see the spill up close and to attempt to bring hope and encouragement to church leaders and those suffering under the weight of this disaster.

All I had said in this book seemed to be challenged by what has happened. I believe that God can redeem all things, that what is broken God seeks to fix, and that he uses his people, his church, to bring restorative justice to all things that are broken. It's true. I look at a broken-down home that has housed crack addicts and drug dealers and prostitutes, that has been a sore in the community, and I see what it can be. I believe that people of faith can tear down this house and build a park or a garden or a playground. They can make what was broken and painful into a source of beauty in a community. I can see it. But I have to be honest; in some ways I believe that this might be possible without a miraculous intervention from God. I believe it's inspired by God; I believe that God helps us along the way, gives us eyes to see, and gives us vision to pursue this new reality, this new Kingdom. But as I looked at the oil spill it became perfectly clear that for this ocean to be restored, for this landmass of the gulf coast and its broad shores to be healed so that the people of Louisiana and far beyond can return to their occupations, it would take a miracle from the very hand of God.

So it was only fitting, when we gathered the residents of the Gulf Coast together, that we would gather for an evening of prayer. I wondered what I would pray. What words of encouragement could

I offer? Would they be guarded? Pessimistic? What I sensed from the Spirit was a hope that could only come from God.

We gathered in a church on the east end of New Orleans that was devastated by Hurricane Katrina. The worship center was under more than eight feet of water after that storm, and the church, which had already been struggling before, seemed to face an inevitable death after the hurricane's destruction. But through the storm, God brought about something beautiful. Two struggling congregations—a historically white congregation and a historically black congregation—made a radical decision that they both needed one another and that together they could do something they could not do apart. They came into the wrecked church building and began to restore it together. They began to worship together, and you can imagine how their worship experienced a new kind of vibrancy and diversity and beauty—a new kind of passion for their city and their neighbors.

As I faced my own doubt and disbelief that God could step in and restore such a tragic event in the Gulf Coast, I sat in a new chair in a beautifully renovated sanctuary, with an African American gospel choir, next to white ninety-year-old grandmother who, throughout the service, would quietly rub lotion on her crumpled arthritic hands. In that place, I was reminded of the beauty in the truth that God is restoring all things. Those who give up will fail to see the ultimate redemptive power of our living, loving, and restoring God.

Throughout the evening we prayed for those who are suffering—for fishermen, for churches, for the rural people who rely on the ocean for its seafood, for those who work in restaurants that serve that seafood. And as the evening built, we sensed our faith continuing to grow with a belief that God would bring us together in the midst of this tragedy in a way that would change all of us, and ultimately change the Gulf Coast communities and the waters themselves. I believe God is up to something beautiful and magnificent, and that God will ultimately bring all of us, and many others, together in the years that follow the spill. We'll be able to look back and see the ways God orchestrated what never would have been possible without this tragedy.

I believe that one day we'll live in a world that is less dependent on fossil fuels, that we will find cleaner energy sources, that congregations will work together to care for the earth, that the clean up efforts will unify churches and people. I believe this will make us able to see and appreciate the beauty of God's creation in a new way. I believe people will come to faith in Jesus as they witness the testimony of churches rising up to be who they are called to be.

I invite you to gather your friends and discuss these truths together. Maybe you can visit the Gulf Coast to be part of the restorative work; but I also remind you that there are crack houses and bankrupt schools in the poor neighborhoods near your home. There are those in jail who are suffering and longing for someone to visit them or welcome them when they are paroled and given a fresh chance. I pray that God begins his work within us and calls us to seek first his kingdom—a place where shalom and wholeness are restored—and that together we will move toward his righteousness, his ability to restore all things that are broken on this earth. Amen.

Acknowledgments

To my family: Lisa, Hanna, Trinity, Solomon, and Christian; you make life so much fun.

I am so grateful for siblings that are my dearest friends; Brian, Jennifer, Robbie, and Jessica you are the best.

To Sam Rowen: I am so grateful for your help on this project.

Greg Garrett, you are not only a great friend, you are also a priceless resource to me as a writer.

Ecclesia, it is a privilege to serve you as we seek to see the gospel of our Liberating King change the world. Thank you for believing in miracles and looking for the best in other people. I love you all!

J. Wakeham, Tyler Young, and Kelly Hall, thanks for your help, encouragement, and keen eye for my mistakes.

Thanks to Steven Hicks, Elizabeth Puente, Jeremy Wells, John Starr, Paul Randall, Manuel Sanchez, Tiffany Kantas, Wayne Brown,

David Capes, Jack Wisdom, Gideon Tsang, RSB, and so many others who have picked up on so many things during the writing of this book.

My amazing agent Esther Fedorkevich, I am so grateful for your partnership on this and many future projects.

To my publisher, Matt Baugher: it has been a joy working with you. I am also grateful to the entire Thomas Nelson family, namely Mike Hyatt, Frank Couch, Maleah Bell, Emily Sweeney, Jennifer McNeil, Stephanie Newton, Kelly Hughes, and many others who work faithfully to get books and Bibles printed and available for sale in so many stores.

Rick McKinley, Greg Holder, and all the Advent Conspirators, I pray that we all continue to Worship Fully, Spend Less, Give More, and Love All!

Ecclesia Bible Society and all the team working on The Voice, your hard work in bringing the Scriptures to life for those who may have never heard this good news is forever appreciated.

To Sky Bar in Galveston: your sushi was the fuel that made this project a reality. I am also grateful to other who shared good food to keep me writing, especially Pappasitos, The Houstonian, Pointe West, Taft Street Coffee, Mai's, T'Afia, Jasper's, Doyle's, and Tia Maria's. Thanks for allowing me to eat and write at your fine establishments.

Finally to Scott Erickson: collaborating with you is one of the great joys of my life. Thanks for donating your art to enhance the message and clarity of this book.

Analysis of Barna Research

by David Kinnaman, President, Barna Group

Background

Chris Seay and the publisher of this book, Thomas Nelson, asked our company, Barna Group, to explore what Americans think about righteousness. This book includes this exclusive research, described in chapter 1. You can download a free copy of the full Barna research report, including additional findings, at www.chrisseay.com.

Study details

The research for *The Gospel According to Jesus* was conducted in January and February 2010. It relied upon the Barna Group's OmniPollSM—a nationwide study of American adults. The study included random, representative telephone interviews among 1005 adults, including 857 self-identified Christians and 502 churchgoers. (The sampling error associated with Christians is plus or minus 3.3 percentage points, and the sampling error for churchgoers is plus or minus 4.4 percentage points, at the 95% confidence level.)

In the study, several questions were used to probe people's attitudes on the matter. The first was a closed-ended question asking whether respondents had ever heard of or were familiar with the term *righteousness*. Among those familiar with the term, a follow-up closed-ended question probed what people thought Jesus was referring to when he talked about seeking first the kingdom of God. Survey respondents were given five different words from which to select: *holiness, faithfulness, morality, justice,* and *beauty*.

Findings

The responses can be analyzed from two different points of view. The first view is based on the first word selected by respondents (often referred to by researchers, cleverly, as "first response"). This is a forced-choice scenario, in which people are asked to select the word that comes closest to describing their knowledge of the term. The second point of view on the data is the "all response" scenario, in which respondents were given the chance to mention as many options as they liked, and this data reflects the frequency with which they selected each word.

On the basis of the first response point of view, we learned that *holiness* (32 percent) and *faithfulness* (29 percent) are the most common words that Christians select to describe the meaning of Matthew 6:33. This is followed by *morality* (17 percent), rounded out by *justice* (6 percent), and *beauty* (2 percent). Another 6 percent of respondents said *something else* was in Jesus' mind in Matthew 6:33; another 7 percent answered *not sure*.

When given the chance to give multiple responses, *holiness* and *faithfulness* got even more votes, increasing to 52 percent and 53 percent respectively. The same was the case for *morality* (35 percent), *justice* (26 percent), and *beauty* (14 percent).

Implications

Americans maintain some residual awareness of the term *righteousness*, but few admit that they are really all that familiar with the concept. It is a phrase that most Christians have heard of, but it has lost—if it ever had—any real meaning to Christ followers.

What is more, American Christians put a works-based perspective on the concept of righteousness. For instance, in the research for the book *unChristian*, we found most believers in this nation define Christianity as not sinning and being a good person. But focusing on behavior, rules, and sin avoidance ends up creating many people who come across as pretentious, hollow, and even *self-righteous*.

In fact, I believe, based on the research, many of us Christians are stuck in self-righteous lives because we don't understand what Jesus really meant by righteousness. We all need to think more deeply about the upside-down way of life taught by Jesus.

Yet, despite some of the uncomfortable findings of the project we conducted for Chris Seay, I was also encouraged by the research; we found that most Christians actually tend to believe that righteousness is *multi-faceted and multi-dimensional*. Typically, we find that multiple-response questions only inspire a little extra response—as though people cannot wait to move on in the survey. Yet respondents to this question were quite willing to select many different words from the list of five to describe righteousness. In other words, the encouraging news is that Christians want a description of righteousness that is both theologically rich and plainly livable.

David Kinnaman
Ventura, California

Notes

Chapter 1

1. Ralph Winter, "Reconsecration to a Wartime, not a Peacetime, Lifestyle," in *Perspectives on the World Christian Movement: A Reader*, 2nd edition, eds. Ralph D. Winter and Steven C. Hawthorne (Pasadena, CA: William Carey Library, 1999), 706.
2. Mark Batterson, *Primal: A Quest for the Lost Soul of Christianity* (Colorado Springs, CO: Multnomah, 2009), 143.

Chapter 2

1. See Matthew 6:25–34.
2. Matt Tittle, "My Visit to Ecclesia," Keep the Faith Blog, http://blogs.chron.com/keepthefaith/2009/07/my_visit_to_ecclesia.html.
3. Will L. Thompson, "Softly and Tenderly," public domain.
4. Literally, "John who immersed, to show repentance."

Notes

Chapter 3

1. Lesslie Newbigin, *Signs amid the Rubble: The Purposes of God in Human History*, ed. Geoffrey Wainwright (Grand Rapids, MI: Eerdmans, 2003), 115.
2. Ibid., 99.
3. Pope Benedict XVI, *Jesus of Nazareth* (San Francisco: Ignatius Press, 2008), 46–47.
4. William Tyndale, "A Pathway Into the Holy Scripture," in *Doctrinal Treatises*, ed. Henry Walter (Cambridge, MA: Cambridge University Press, 1531/1848), 8–9.
5. D. A. Carson, "The Biblical Gospel," *For Such a Time as This: Perspectives on Evangelicalism, Past, Present and Future*, eds. Steve Brady and Harold Rowdon (London: Evangelical Alliance, 1996), 6.
6. Ibid., 6.
7. Tim Keller, "Redeemer's Core Commitments," Redeemer Presbyterian Church, http://redeemerpres.com/content/view/15/30/.
8. Rick McKinley, "The Gospel and the Kingdom," The Gospel in Action Blog, http://extendingthekingdom.org/?page_id=20.
9. Martin Luther, *Martin Luther's Basic Theological Writings*, eds. Timothy F. Lull and William R. Russell (Minneapolis: Augsburg Fortress, 2005), 94.
10. See Habakkuk 2:4.
11. Luther, *Martin Luther's Basic Theological Writings*, 94.

Chapter 4

1. Carl Sagan, "A Gift for Vividness," *Time*, October 20, 1980, 61.
2. See Genesis 2:9.
3. The earliest manuscripts omit this portion of Romans 8:1.
4. Walter Brueggemann, video interview, "The Work of the People," http://www.theworkofthepeople.com/index.php?ct=store.details&pid=V00587.

Chapter 5

1. Interview with N. T. Wright, October 2005, http://www.ntwrightpage.com/Wrightsaid_October2005.htm.
2. Matt Jenson, *The Gravity of Sin: Augustine, Luther and Barth on Homo Incurvatus in Se*, (London: T&T Clark, 2007), 2.
3. Christine Wicker, "Dumbfounded by Divorce," *Dallas Morning News*, 2000, http://www.adherents.com/largecom/baptist_divorce.html.
4. Dallas Willard, *The Divine Conspiracy: Rediscovering Our Hidden Life in God* (New York: HarperOne, 1998), 40.
5. Ibid., 41.

Chapter 6

1. Donald Miller, *Blue Like Jazz: Nonreligious Thoughts on Christian Spirituality* (Nashville: Thomas Nelson, 2003), 20.
2. *Lost* (ABC), "Confidence Man," originally aired November 11, 2004.
3. Martin Luther, "The Large Catechism of Martin Luther", trans. F. Bente and W. H. T. Dau, *Triglot Concordia: The Symbolical Books of the Ev. Lutheran Church* (St. Louis: Concordia Publishing House, 1921), as printed on the Project Wittenberg Web site, http://www.iclnet.org/pub/resources/text/wittenberg/luther/catechism/web/cat-03.html.
4. Ed Clowney, "Revelation of God's Wrath Against the Moralists" (sermon), http://www.sermonaudio.com/sermoninfo.asp?SID=1121071349130.

Chapter 7

1. "Announcing MarkeTips' Apollo 13 Duct Tape Challenge," MarkeTips, November/December 2002, http://www.fss.gsa.gov/pub/mtips/Nov_Dec02/Duct_Tape.pdf.
2. Dr. C. Matthew McMahon, "Justification by Faith Alone: A Plea for Understanding," http://www.apuritansmind.com/Justification/JustificationMainPage.htm.
3. John MacArthur, "Scripture, Tradition, and Rome, Part 4: Long Before Luther; Jesus and the Doctrine of Justification," http://www.gty.org/Resources/Articles/A247_Scripture-Tradition-and-Rome-Part-4?q=.
4. Interview with N. T. Wright, Thursday, November 15, 2007, Asbury Seminary.
5. John Howard Yoder, *The Politics of Jesus* (Grand Rapids, MI: Eerdmans, 1994), 224.
6. UNICEF, The State of the World's Children, 1999, http://www.unicef.org/sowc99.
7. United Nations Development Program, 2007 Human Development Report (HDR), November 27th, 2007, 2.
8. Anup Shah, "Today, Over 24,000 Children Died Around the World," Global Issues.org, http://www.globalissues.org/article/715/today-over-24000-children-died-around-the-world. (Note that the statistic cited uses children as those under the age of five. If it were under the age of, say, six or seven, the numbers would be even higher.)
9. UNICEF, "Orphans," http://www.unicef.org/media/media_45290.html.
10. "Orphan Statistics," http://skywardjourney.wordpress.com/orphan-statistics/.

Chapter 8

1. Christine Aroney-Sine, *Wholeness & the Shalom of God* (unpublished manuscript, Mustard Seed Associates, 2001), 11.
2. Some ancient manuscripts omit the end of verse 3 and all of verse 4.
3. See Isaiah 61:1–2.
4. Abraham J. Heschel, *The Prophets* (New York: Harper & Row, 1962), 3-4.
5. Greg Garrett, *Holy Superheroes! Exploring the Sacred in Comics, Graphic Novels, and Film,* revised and expanded edition (Louisville: Westminster John Knox, 2009), 43.

Chapter 9

1. Mother Teresa, to Rev. Michael van der Peet, September 1979, from Brian Kolodiejchuck, *Mother Teresa: Come Be My Light: The Private Writings of the Saint of Calcutta* (New York: Doubleday Religion, 2007).
2. A Greek *lepta*, a coin worth an insignificant amount.
3. Visit www.rescuebabiesnow.org.

About the Author

CHRIS SEAY is a church planter, pastor, president of Ecclesia Bible Society, and internationally acclaimed speaker. His six previous books include *The Gospel According to* Lost, *The Gospel According to Tony Soprano*, and *Faith of My Fathers*.

Blog: www.therestorativejustice.com

Twitter: PastorChrisSeay

Church/Podcasts: www.ecclesiahouston.org

A Project to Rediscover the Bible

The Scripture quotations in *The Gospel According to Jesus* have been taken from *The Voice™*.

A collaboration between scholars, writers, musicians, and other artists to bring the Bible to life.

The Voice™ is a fresh expression of the timeless narrative known as the Bible. Too often the passion, grit, humor, and beauty has been lost in the translation process. *The Voice™* seeks to recapture what was lost.

To learn more, visit www.hearthevoice.com.

Available wherever books & Bibles are sold

An Epic journey
into the deepest mysteries of faith

The Gospel According to Lost explores each element of the hit show in an analysis of faith of metaphor—a perfect resource for those who want to go even deeper into the journey.

Inside, you'll discover what *Lost* has to say about:

- the clash between faith and reason, on the island and in real life;

- the struggle with guilt that consumes each character—and sometimes us too;

- the dichotomy between fatalism and fate, and what the Bible advises;

- how being lost—on an island or in society—presents an opportunity for reinvention that liberates some and paralyzes others.

Available wherever books and e-books are sold
www.thomasnelson.com

The images in *The Gospel According to Jesus*

are original paintings by Scott Erickson,

studio artist and experiential artist in

residence at Ecclesia Church in Houston.

To learn more about Scott and his work,

visit www.scottericksonart.com.